CW01456566

SHAKESPEARE'S

Hamlet

Peter Davies

GE

GREENWICH EXCHANGE
LONDON

Greenwich Exchange, London

Shakespeare's *Hamlet*

© Peter Davies 2008

First published in Great Britain in 2008
All rights reserved

This book is sold subject to the conditions that it shall not, by way of
trade or otherwise, be lent, resold, hired out, or otherwise circulated
without the publisher's prior consent in any form of binding or cover
other than that in which it is published and without a similar condition
including this condition being imposed on the subsequent purchaser.

Printed and bound by Q3 Digital/Litho, Loughborough
Tel: 01509 213456
Typesetting and layout by Albion Associates, London
Tel: 020 8852 4646
Cover design by December Publications, Belfast
Tel: 028 90286559

Cover Image: Sam West as Hamlet, 2001.
Photo by Alastair Thain: © RSC

Greenwich Exchange Website: www.greenex.co.uk

Cataloguing in Publication Data is available from the British Library

ISBN-13: 978-1-906075-12-5
ISBN-10: 1-906075-12-3

to
Antonia, Joanna
and
Justine

Contents

Introduction

Date and text

Hamlet offers us one of the most bedevilled of all Shakespeare's texts. The early editions of it vary widely, and the date of its composition is also unclear. Judged purely from internal evidence, principally its tendency even in its moments of greatest tension to a still youthful lyric grace, it feels like a play from the earlier part of Shakespeare's maturity, evidently coming ahead of the more sombre *Othello*, *King Lear* and *Macbeth*. That much is ascertainable from the records available to us. The play was first entered in the Register of the Stationers' Company on 26th July 1602 by James Roberts. Shakespeare's reference (in the mouth of Hamlet, as he talks to the actors) to "an eyrie of children, little eyases, that cry out on the top of question, and are most tyrannically clapped for't. These are now the fashion, and so berattle the common stages ..." (Act II, scene 2, 338ff) is surely a rueful, not to say indignant, allusion to the boy actors established at the rival Blackfriars Theatre at Christmas 1600, and making an immediate impact on audiences. A new style of – somewhat facile? – vivacity is coming into vogue, and this does not please a Shakespeare who is entering on the most serious phase of his creative life.

Be that as it may, an edition of the play does not appear until 1603, an edition printed by Valentine Simmes, who had printed a number of Shakespeare's previous plays. This is the notorious First Quarto (Q1), condemned to be known ever after as "the bad Quarto". Well, there is ample justification for that. It has all the hallmarks of an edition that was rushed into print, and not even from a prompt copy, which would certainly have had a bedrock of accuracy about it, but from the (imperfect) rememberings of a member of the cast, who, impelled by the immense success of the first performances, could not wait for the due process of publication – always a lackadaisical process with Shakespeare – but jotted down what he thought he had heard, rushed out and sold the result to the highest bidder. The sonorous title of this lash-up was *The Tragicall Historie of Hamlet, Prince of Denmarke*. And it was also described on the title page as having been "diverse times acted by his Highnesse servants in the Cittie of London: and also in the two Universities of Cambridge and Oxford, and elsewhere." The reference to "his Highnesse servants" clearly indicates the point, sometime in May 1603, at which the Lord Chamberlain's Men, Shakespeare's company since 1594, came under the patronage of the new king, James I, and became the King's Men. They now played frequently at court, but there is no other reference to their ever having performed at Oxford or Cambridge.

The actor who first played Marcellus has traditionally fallen under suspicion for this act of piracy – largely because, though so much of the text of Q1 is botched up, the lines of Marcellus seem to have come over almost flawlessly. "Marcellus" (who only appears in Act I – unless he happened to double as Osrick later on) has also failed to remember vast chunks of the text. The "bad" Quarto contains only 2,200 lines. Its successor, the Second Quarto (Q2), has 3,800. But it is not just a matter of quantity. The quality of the actor's recollections is desperately poor – again suggesting that he had a relatively minor part.

In any event, a brief sampling of Q1 will serve to show what a shoddy job its first enterprising pirate editor made of Shakespeare's play. The famous soliloquy of Act III, scene 1:

> To be, or not to be – that is the question;
> Whether 'tis nobler in the mind to suffer
> The slings and arrows of outrageous fortune
> Or to take arms against a sea of troubles
> And by opposing end them. To die, to sleep –
> No more …

has become:

> To be, or not to be, I there's the point,
> To Die, to sleepe, is that all? I all:
> No, to sleepe, to dreame, I mary, there it goes,

For in that dreame of death, when wee awake,
And borne before an everlasting judge,
From whence no passenger ever return'd,
The undiscovered country, at whose sight
The happy smile and the accursed damn'd.

It seems fair to say that it could only have been a bit-part actor who turned Shakespeare's marvellous poetry into such illiterate doggerel. A man who had been in daily, prolonged contact with the verse of the play's great speeches in rehearsal and performance must surely have developed some understanding of what the lines meant. The thought that this 'editor' might never have had more scrupulous successors to rectify his wrongs is enough to send shivers down the spine. It gives some inkling of the enormous task that faces Shakespeare's modern editors. However, like certain other plays of Shakespeare, notably *Romeo and Juliet*, the text of *Hamlet* survived this first disastrous outing to go on to better things.

Whether or not the Chamberlain's Men, turned King's Men, took fright at the thought of this bowdlerised version masquerading in circulation as their piece of intellectual property, we do not know. In any event, Q2, printed by James Roberts, appeared in 1604, and is clearly an 'authorised' publication. This version of The *Tragicall History of Hamlet, Prince of Denmarke*, is pointedly described on the title page as being "Newly imprinted and enlarged to almost as much againe as it was, according to the true and perfect Coppie".

True and perfect copy it certainly is not. Thanks to the difficulty in reading the handwriting of what may well have been Shakespeare's original, it is full of misprints and is atrociously punctuated. But it has, in full, all the philosophical digressions that are missing from Q1. It provided the basis for performance until the appearance of the First Folio edition (F1) of Shakespeare's works, edited by John Heminge and Henry Condell and published in 1623, after the playwright's death. Between them Q2 and F1 (which besides adding matter that is not in Q2, omits lines that by 1623 might commonly have been cut in performance, and corrects Q2's many mistakes) provide the basis for the work of modern editors. The 'bad' Q1, with all its imperfections, has its uses. Its stage directions are interesting in that they are 'hot' from stage performance. And it can occasionally help with a reading that is still confusing in Q2 and F1.

Shakespeare's sources for *Hamlet*

The *Historiae Danicae* of Saxo Grammaticus, a 12th-century Danish historian, is the first extant account of the story of Hamlet. It is a frankly crude tale from the age of the sagas (though a good way below them in terms of artistic merit), and is undoubtedly based on legends existing from an age before Saxo. In it, Horwendil (= old Hamlet) rules Jutland as a vassal of Roric King of Denmark, with his brother Fengo (= Claudius). Through his martial prowess, he gains Roric's favour and his daughter Gerutha (= Gertrude), by whom he has a son Amleth (= Hamlet). Fengo, jealous of his brother's deeds (which include slaying the King of Norway (= Old Fortinbras), kills his brother and marries Gerutha. Young Amleth, fearful for his own life, feigns madness while he contemplates revenge, and after a series of adventures, many of which in one form or other find their way into Shakespeare's play, kills Fengo and is acclaimed king. Saxo's account takes the Hamlet story much further, with many more layers of adventure befalling its protagonist, until he meets his own heroic death.

The *Historiae Danicae* was first published in Paris in 1514. All the elements of Shakespeare's play are there: fratricide, incest, feigned madness. But it is highly doubtful that Shakespeare, with his "small Latin and less Greek" had read it. Nevertheless it was known to readers in Tudor England through a version in French, *Histoires Tragiques*, by the prolific author, poet and translator François de Belleforest, published between 1559 and 1582. This contains all the details of the Saxo story and adds a few of its own for good measure, the whole thing being spun out to almost twice Saxo's length. In Belleforest – though not in Saxo – Fengo has committed adultery with Gerutha ("incestueusement soüillé la couche fraternelle") before killing her husband. We shall come later to the question of whether or not Shakespeare means this to have happened in his version of events. It seems to me to be of fundamental importance to any consideration of the degree of Gertrude's guilt/ wrongdoing in Shakespeare's play, and has been much discussed.

How much French did Shakespeare have? Possibly not a great deal from his country grammar school. Certainly not enough to wade with any comfort through the many prolix volumes of Belleforest. There was a contemporary English translation of Belleforest, *The*

Hystorie of Hamblet, but its arrival in 1608 would have been too late for it to have been any use to Shakespeare. Indeed, in a number of details it shows clear signs of having been influenced by his play. This brings us to the vexed question of the famous (through its sheer elusiveness) *Ur-Hamlet* – the Play that Never Was. *Ur-Hamlet* has become something of an evolutionary 'missing link', the discussion of which has been meat and drink to scholars down the ages. By common consent (since Shakespeare would not have been able to gain access to either Saxo or Belleforest), the immediate source for Shakespeare's play must have been a play which itself no longer exists. If this seems a somewhat inconveniently gnomic state of affairs, then there is general agreement that it was being performed and was well known to audiences, as well as being much derided by fellow playwrights, in the years before the period that Shakespeare's play made its appearance. There is not – perhaps never was – a printed text. Nevertheless there is copious reference to it in contemporary sources.

Both Thomas Lodge and Thomas Nashe refer to it. It seems to have been a somewhat ham-fisted, gory piece of revenge tragedy in the Senecan mould, a genre enthusiastically embraced by the Elizabethan stage since the appearance of Thomas Sackville and Thomas Norton's *Gorboduc* in 1561. "Seneca, let blood line by line and page by page, at length must needs die to our stage" is Nashe's somewhat contemptuous verdict on this play, in the preface he wrote to his friend Robert Greene's, very different, euphuistic romance *Menaphon*, which appeared in 1589. From other remarks in this tirade it appears that the composer of this piece, with its "whole Hamlets, I should say handfuls of tragicall speeches", was the son of a scrivener, whose technique "makes his famished followers to imitate the kid in *Aesop*," and who later gave up trying to imitate Seneca to "intermeddle with Italian Translations".

The pointers in this unsubtle piece of ridicule, which is utterly characteristic of the lofty attitude of university wits to mere grammar school boys (Shakespeare was himself to be lampooned by Greene in similar terms), surely clearly identify Thomas Kyd. The clumsy reference to his name apart, he ticks all the boxes: he was a scrivener's son who gave up imitating Seneca to devote himself to translations from the Italian which were then in fashion. His play *Spanish Tragedy* had been perhaps the most triumphantly successful example of the Senecan revenge drama on the English stage. Like Shakespeare, Kyd had no need of Latin to score a tremendous hit with it in London. Its popularity here clearly grates on the scholarly Nashe. A performance of the Kyd *Hamlet* (if Kyd's it was) is mentioned by the theatre manager Philip Henslowe in his *Diary* of 1594. In 1596 Lodge referred to "the ghost which cried so miserably at the theatre, like an oyster-wife, Hamlet, revenge!"

Or was Shakespeare himself, perhaps, the author of the *Ur-Hamlet*? And might the play we have today simply be a reworking and an evolution of an earlier version? A number of scholars of impeccable orthodoxy, led by Peter Alexander and supported by Harold Bloom, have asserted this to be the case. I think the evidence must be against it. Nowhere else in contemporary commentary is an earlier Shakespeare *Hamlet* alluded to. And the pathetic squeaking figure of the ghost referred to by Lodge gives the game away. One of Shakespeare's many achievements was to transform the comic ghost of these early Senecan Elizabethan dramas into a terrifying spiritual phenomenon. That process reaches its apogee with the appearance of old Hamlet on the stage. But it has already begun the early 1590s, in such a play as *King Richard III*.

There is no need to labour the point. There evidently was an *Ur-Hamlet* and, even discounting the jealous scorn of Nashe, it was evidently revenge tragedy of a fairly primitive sort. Shakespeare, by contrast, took the story which had descended from Saxo's gloomy northern tale and transformed it into a polished drama reflecting the many-sided intellectual and moral passion of a sophisticated renaissance sensibility.

This edition

The text on which this Greenwich Exchange Student Guide is based was first published in Penguin Books in 1980, edited by T.J.B. Spencer (who died two years earlier, having completed his work). The quite excellent notes contained in the commentary are also by Spencer. The edition was reprinted with a revised Further Reading in 1996, and reissued in 2005 as the Penguin Shakespeare, and has a critical introduction by Alan Sinfield. It is the edition used and recommended by the National Theatre.

There is only one instance (Act I, scene 1, 63) in which I have deviated in quotation from Spencer's text – but I have made the reasons for this abundantly clear in a discussion on the possible meanings of that line, in Chapter 5.

1

Hamlet and *Hamlet*

Hamlet is, I suppose, the most talked-about play in the entire Shakespeare canon, and Hamlet himself Shakespeare's most discussed protagonist. No character in a Shakespeare play has been analysed to the degree Hamlet has – not merely as a character in a play, but as if he were a real person. There are obvious reasons for this. Of the four great tragedies, *Hamlet* presents us – the supernatural element notwithstanding – with the most recognisably 'human' of problems. The protagonists of *Othello*, *Macbeth* and *King Lear* are mature men, out of the common sphere, at the height of their powers and either on their way to the pinnacle of their careers, or, as in Lear's case, at that summit and on the point of relinquishing it.

But though apparently an heir to a throne, Hamlet is a young man, and still a student when *Hamlet* opens. We first see him in the council chamber of Denmark in a situation in which he is manifestly subordinate to the will of his stepfather and the desires of his mother. When the king, his stepfather, has disposed of the business of state and turns to family matters, it is not Hamlet to whom he first addresses himself, but Laertes, the son of his chief counsellor – not even a family relation. Hamlet, sitting aside, broods meanwhile over a problem that is doubtless common to any age, but seems particularly relevant in one like ours, fascinated as we are with the psycho-dynamics of family life. His father whom he loved and admired – and who was admired by all around him – has died suddenly and unexpectedly. His mother, who doted on his father, has quite inexplicably, and in an indecently short space of time by any standards, married a man whom Hamlet loathes and holds in contempt.

Hamlet is, to be sure, not a troubled teenager. At around thirty he ranks as a somewhat mature student. Nevertheless, before we are even made aware of the other dimensions of the play, we know that we are at the centre of a family drama whose basic elements are familiar to us. A son's long-held assumptions about the affections and sound judgement of his own mother have been destroyed almost in an instant. We do not have to transport ourselves to the mores of a far-off time or country, to feel ourselves in instinctive sympathy with the predicament of the young Hamlet. For Elizabethan audiences – indeed for audiences for almost three centuries afterwards – the natural distaste at Gertrude's actions that we feel would have been compounded by the horror of knowing that her second marriage was an incestuous one.

It is hardly surprising, then, that the Romantic Movement, with its discovery and glorification of the sanctity of the individual, took Hamlet to itself. The rational 18th century had tended to feel uneasy with him. The author of *Some Remarks on the Tragedy of Hamlet* (1736), which is generally ascribed to Thomas Hanmer, was not at all happy with Hamlet's tactic of feigning madness, and also took "great Offence" at the speech he delivers upon catching his uncle at prayer. "There is something so very Bloody in it, so inhuman, so unworthy of a Hero, that I wish our Poet had omitted it." In his *Dissertation sur la Tragédie* of 1748 Voltaire (who in any case thought Shakespeare beyond the pale for his failure to adhere to the dramatic unities prescribed by Aristotle and religiously observed by French dramatists) regarded the play as "a vulgar and barbarous drama, which would not be tolerated by the vilest populace of France, or Italy". Samuel Johnson, while in general an admirer of Shakespeare's work, (even when, as in *King Lear*, he found it too painful to bear) accused him in his 1765 edition of the plays of "having shewn little regard to poetical justice", and charged him with "equal neglect of poetical probability".

The Romantic Movement jettisoned this scepticism. At what seemed to be the dawn of new freedoms for humanity with the overthrow of the despotic *Ancien Regime* in France, it was happy to project its preoccupations onto Shakespeare's hero. To Goethe he was the embodiment of his own creation, Werther, a man of sorrows. Goethe's Hamlet was, as described in *Wilhelm Meister's Apprentice-*

ship (1795–6), "A lovely, pure, noble and most moral nature, without the strength of nerve which forms a hero," and for whom "the present is too hard". That great admirer of Shakespeare, August Wilhelm Schlegel, whose translations into German set a benchmark for excellence, had to confess in his *Dramatic Art and Literature* (1809–11) that he could not "pronounce altogether so favourable a sentence upon it [Hamlet's character] as Goethe does". But he went on perceptively to analyse the realistic co-existence in Hamlet's makeup of "royal manners" and "noble ambition" with "caustic wit" and "a natural inclination for crooked ways". Like Goethe, Schlegel regarded Hamlet as being "too much overwhelmed with his own sorrow to have any compassion to spare for others".

The tendency to see Hamlet in terms that take him out of his play and ascribe to him the attributes of a living being reaches its height in the enthusiasms of such English critics of the early 19th century as William Hazlitt and the poet Samuel Taylor Coleridge. It made the character of Hamlet the one, above all, in which actors strove to excel thereafter, as being the great opportunity to bring alive a recognisable and 'real' man on the stage. In his *Characters of Shakespear's* [sic] *Plays* (1817) Hazlitt gave this eloquent testimony to the sense of universal humanity to be found in Shakespeare's creation: "It is *we* who are Hamlet ..." and proceeded to list a series of circumstances from everyday life (largely those of misfortune) in which the individual might draw strength from the knowledge that he was sharing the experience of Shakespeare's hero. Coleridge personalised the "Hamlet experience" even further, glorying in the paralysis of action that must necessarily afflict those of philosophical, as opposed to practical, habits of mind and concluding: "I have a smack of Hamlet in myself, if I may say so."

From that time on, much aided by the rise of the English novel and its tendency to encourage literal realism in the analysis of literary character, the process of turning Hamlet into a character whom we might encounter among us on any day, anywhere, was completed. His problems had an echo in ours. In particular, his famous melancholy was increasingly analysed in Victorian times, in terms of a developing understanding of mental illness, as opposed to moral poisoning.

As the 19th century turned into the 20th, Freudian psychoanalysis lent its weight to the process of criticism. Freud's own opinion that Hamlet suffered from an Oedipus complex was explored by his Welsh disciple, Ernest Jones, the neurologist and president of the International Psychoanalytical Association. Although Dr Jones was not, in his book *Hamlet and Oedipus* (1949), able to point to a sexual relationship (or desire for one) between Hamlet and his mother, he did explore the idea that Hamlet had in fact been as jealous of his father as of his stepfather as rivals for his mother's love for him. In Jones's analysis, the victim of the fallout of the misogyny to which this powerful feeling had given rise was the unfortunate Ophelia, who remained quite unconscious of the fact that Hamlet's bitter outburst against her was really directed against his mother.

As a survey of these developments suggests, the process of identifying the Renaissance man Hamlet with a whole series of modern mental conditions and neuroses, was not necessarily the same thing as conferring continuing approval on him. The venerable A.C. Bradley (*Shakespearean Tragedy*, 1904), a critic whose stock has deservedly been rising in more recent times after a period of neglect in the second half of the last century, deplored Hamlet's bad manners to both Claudius and Polonius, deprecated his "cruelty to Ophelia …", particularly "the disgusting and insulting language to her in the play scene", and quaintly objected to the "insensibility in Hamlet's language about the fate of Rosencrantz and Guildenstern" (who just happen to have been bearing the captive Hamlet and his death warrant to England).

An equally eminent critic of not dissimilar sensibility (and strong Christian belief), G. Wilson Knight, wrote in his famous study *The Wheel of Fire* (1930) of the "demon of cynicism, and its logical result of callous cruelty, that has Hamlet's soul in its remorseless grip". In Wilson Knight's reading, Hamlet has become "an element of evil in the state of Denmark" – presumably in contrast with "… the wise and considerate Claudius, the affectionate mother Gertrude, the eminently lovable old Polonius".

Add to these combative verdicts, stage and movie treatments of the role as varied as Laurence Olivier's dignified film performance of 1948; David Warner's neurotic student of the Royal Shakespeare Company's 1965 stage production; the sheer endurance test of Kenneth Branagh's hyper-dramatic portrayal in his uncut film version of 1996; Ethan Hawke's manipulative CEO of Denmark Corp in the ingenious Michael Almereyda movie of 2000; and Sam West's intelligent rebel in the 2001 Ben Pimlott RSC production, and it apparently becomes possible to concede, as has so often been said, that "there are as many Hamlets as there are actors to play the part" – and, one might add, commentators to comment on it. But is that the same thing as saying that in creating Hamlet Shakespeare wrote a blank cheque? Is Hamlet's creator to blame for what the Earl of Shaftesbury identified as the play's unusual problem as early as 1710, namely that it had "only ONE character".

As Andrew Dickson points out (*The Rough Guide to Shakespeare*, 2005) "with over 1,500 lines, almost half as much again as *Richard III*, the Danish prince is the most voluble character in Shakespeare". But how many of these lines are devoted to the kind of self-analysis of the kind we associate with the protagonist of a modern, psychological novel? Dickson goes on to observe that "Some of these 'words' are the most renowned, not just in the canon, but in the language."

The fact is that *Hamlet* is an extraordinarily philosophical play. In contemplating the apparently simple task of avenging his father's murder, Hamlet's mind ranges in soliloquy after soliloquy, or in down-to-earth conversations with players and gravediggers, over metaphysical problems which, though rich in suggestion, have absolutely nothing to do with the task in hand. And the extraordinary thing is that scarcely at any point are we aware of the mechanics of delay. An exception *might* be made for "Now might I do it pat" (Act III, scene 3, 73), as Hamlet contemplates killing the praying and defenceless Claudius – but the fact is that we feel no resentment at the failure to "do it pat". Why not? Such a solution would, of course, bring this marvellous play to an end rather prematurely – which would be a pity. But such an end would merely leave us with the successful dénouement to a revenge play. It would not make a tragedy. The play would have been brought to an end without our having a chance fully to comprehend the scale and depth of corruption that Claudius has brought to the Danish court and its denizens, not merely through his having killed a king and married his widow, but through his continuing inability to cease being corrupt, and his capacity, almost to the point of his death, to continue to corrupt those around him.

We have been dogged for more than two centuries by Goethe's view that Hamlet is about "a great action laid upon a soul unfit for the performance of it", i.e. that Hamlet is simply not 'up to' the task of avenging his father. Yet the act of revenge when it (almost incidentally) comes is one of the least important of the several climaxes in the play – although, of course, it never fails to make exciting stage business. *Hamlet* is, surely, not simply the personal tragedy of a man who, as the Olivier film glosses it: "could not make up his mind" – and has it made up for him accidentally at the end? Indecision is hardly the stuff of tragedy. And at the end a body count of eight (excluding Hamlet's father) which includes all the main protagonists, surely asks us to look further afield than that. Have all these people died merely because of some shortcoming in Hamlet? Could the butcher's bill not have been shortened by his simply getting a grip on himself and making a few simple decisions? There seems something preposterous in the suggestion.

Yet some critics have taken Hamlet's fault even further. For the steadfastly anti-Romantic T.S. Eliot (*Selected Essays*, 1932) "Hamlet (the man) is dominated by an emotion which is inexpressible, because it is in *excess* of the facts as they appear."

For Eliot, of course, it is not Hamlet, but *Hamlet* that is at fault. "Few critics have ever admitted that *Hamlet* the play is the primary problem, and Hamlet the character only the secondary." We might be grateful for what appears to be a shift in focus which takes the burden of wrong, and the solution to it, off the shoulders of the protagonist and transfers it elsewhere, if it were not for the fact that Eliot goes on to make it clear that he thinks *Hamlet* is simply a bad play. "So far from being Shakespeare's masterpiece, the play is most certainly an artistic failure." And in furthering this view he went on to expound his famous theory of the 'objective correlative': "The only way of expressing emotion in the form of art is by finding an 'objective correlative'; in other words, a set of objects, a situation, a chain of events which shall be the formula of that *particular* emotion; such that when the external facts, which must terminate in sensory experience, are given, the emotion is immediately evoked."

The theory has been a useful one and crystallizes much about the way in which art works. Eliot finds it working for him in *Macbeth*. There, the emotions of both Macbeth and Lady Macbeth are the natural expression of the sum of their respective experiences. By contrast, for Eliot, *Hamlet* fails the test of artistic 'inevitability'. There is nothing in the experience of its protagonist that can give rise to the weighty charge of emotion which Shakespeare has laid on Hamlet. It is a verdict which drew from Patrick Cruttwell in his essay *The Morality of Hamlet – 'Sweet Prince' or 'Arrant Knave'?* (1963) the, in the circumstances, mild remonstrance: "when I consider all this [i.e. the death of Hamlet's father; the hasty, incestuous remarriage of his mother; his being cheated of the throne; learning from the Ghost of his father that he has in fact been murdered] I find it hard to imagine any degree of emotion which ought to be censured as 'excessive'."

Now we might be inclined to think that something is seriously wrong when such an eminent poet (and playwright) and scholarly critic as Eliot is led to damn, not out of hand but after a scrupulous process of thought, one of Shakespeare's apparently most enduring masterpieces. Eliot was far too serious a man to adopt any position just for effect. Yet, it seems to me that in focusing his dissatisfaction over *Hamlet*, on the play's protagonist, on his emotion and on the excess of it, the classicist Eliot has come close to running himself into the very misunderstanding he deplored in the great Romantics Goethe and Coleridge. Eliot has – dare we say it? – missed the point of *Hamlet*.

For although it is true that in the play we are soon to see Hamlet confronted by problems whose very nature comes close to overwhelming his reason, he is designedly not a participant in the action of the opening scene. Shakespeare does not get these things wrong. If he wants his protagonist to give an account of himself at the outset, or to have others of the dramatis personae sketch some essentials of a character for us, he never finds it difficult to arrange it. In *Othello, King Lear* and *Macbeth* some important aspect of each respective protagonist is laid before us right away, and these act as important pointers to the action. Thus, we immediately learn that Othello is hated, with a lethal hatred, by the very man whom he is supposed to trust, his "honest" ensign, Iago. Macbeth is a valiant servant of the state, but his fate is, from the very first moment of the play, somehow – and mysteriously – bound up with witches. Lear is a hitherto-feared monarch, now seen in a state of volatile indecision, between two powerful sons-in-law about the future of the state whose rule he is about to give up, and this creates a potent sense of unease. The opening of *Hamlet* presents us with something rather different. Hamlet does not appear, nor is his character discussed. His name is not mentioned until the very end of scene 1. Instead we are given a worried discussion on an untoward happening, put in the mouths of a small group of soldiers, keeping an uneasy watch on the ramparts of a citadel on a freezing cold night. It seems clear that Shakespeare intends the focus of our attention at this opening moment of the drama to be not his protagonist, but the state of Denmark itself. And it seems to me that this is the starting point for our inquiry: What is the tragedy of *Hamlet* the play, not Hamlet the man?

2

Something is rotten …

It is not until the last scene of Act I that the Ghost appears to Hamlet to tell him that the man sitting on the throne of Denmark is doing so courtesy of the murder of Hamlet's father. This regicide is, of course, the most colossal of the pieces of information that we receive from the Ghost about the state of affairs in the kingdom. Yet in many ways even this merely sets the seal on a carefully generated sense of unease about the moral condition of Denmark that has hung over the play since its opening scene.

Hamlet begins with a change of the watch on the battlements of the castle at Elsinore. Barnardo is relieving Francisco on the platform, and their exchanges, in keeping with soldierly punctilio, are the unremarkable variants on "Who goes there?" that we would expect on such an occasion. Francisco congratulates Barnardo on his timekeeping, but as he turns to leave he makes the curious remark as an addendum to his thanks: "And I am sick at heart." (Act I, scene 1, 9)

To what, we ask, does this refer? To previous alarming sightings of the Ghost, which have already been discussed among them? Or to the general condition of the state which occasions this watch in the first place? We cannot know, and after he leaves his place of watch Francisco is not seen in the play again. But (and it is characteristic of Shakespeare to touch on a play's major themes obliquely through the mouths of subordinate characters) it undoubtedly foreshadows the soon-to-be-dominating angst of the play's eponymous protagonist.

Horatio, clearly sceptical about the Ghost, now comes on to the platform with Marcellus, and is briefed by Barnardo on their previous sightings, a recital interrupted by the Ghost's appearance. Horatio's reaction to it immediately ratchets up the sense of impending evil: "This bodes some strange eruption to our state." (Act I, scene 1, 69).

This aperçu is an opportunity for Marcellus to tell him about the war psychosis that is, from all appearances, already afflicting Denmark. A reappearance of the Ghost, cutting across Horatio's explanation for all this, serves only, it seems, to confirm some connection between this visitation and the moral health of the country. The apparition leaves the three men in a fog of bewilderment.

We are then, quite out of the blue, confronted with the consummate lyrical beauty of verse exchanges between Marcellus and Horatio, as both men reflect on the Ghost's departure. Shakespeare does not suddenly break into soaring lyrics for nothing. These beautiful lines serve starkly to point up the contrast between the malediction suggested by the wandering spirit's flight at cockcrow "like a guilty thing/Upon a fearful summons" (Act I, scene 1, 149-50) and that "hallowed" season of Christ's birth. In a stroke of genius from Shakespeare it is made to fall to the simple soldier Marcellus to give utterance to a sublimity of thought that lifts us above the dread of this night, the supernatural and the grim preparations for war that beat their drum throughout the scene. The Ghost has gone, day has come, and it is as if the spirit of man breathes again in contemplation of the blessing of Christmas.

> It faded on the crowing of the cock.
> Some say that ever 'gainst that season comes
> Wherein our Saviour's birth is celebrated,
> This bird of dawning singeth all night long.
> And then, they say, no spirit dare stir abroad;
> The nights are wholesome; then no planets strike;
> No fairy takes; nor witch hath power to charm.
> So hallowed and so gracious is that time.
>   (Act I, scene 1, 158-65)

At Christ's nativity malign influences have no power over human beings. That is not so here in Elsinore, where the presence of wickedness has permitted the Ghost to burst his cerements, "making night hideous" with his baneful presence. The dramatic irony of Marcellus's beautiful speech recalls irresistibly the "pleasant seat" and the "temple-haunting martlet" of Macbeth's castle under whose battlements King Duncan, innocent in his commendation of them, passes to be butchered by his host and hostess in the bed they have provided for him. The vision of Marcellus, too, is one of holy innocence that will not be glimpsed again in the play, as evil relentlessly laps about, and then destroys, its protagonists. From this pure atmosphere where men battle with spirits and their own fears in the frosts of a winter's night we are transported in scene 2 to the warm interior of Claudius's court.

KING

> Though yet of Hamlet our dear brother's death
> The memory be green, and that it us befitted
> To bear our hearts in grief, and our whole kingdom
> To be contracted in one brow of woe,
> Yet so far hath discretion fought with nature
> That we with wisest sorrow think on him
> Together with remembrance of ourselves.
> Therefore our sometime sister, now our Queen,
> Th'imperial jointress to this warlike state,
> Have we, as 'twere with a defeated joy,
> With an auspicious and a dropping eye,
> With mirth in funeral and with dirge in marriage,
> In equal scale weighing delight and dole,
> Taken to wife. Nor have we herein barred
> Your better wisdoms, which have freely gone
> With this affair along. For all, our thanks.

(Act I, scene 2, 1-16)

The ethos is that of the council chamber. The minutes of the last meeting have, as it were, been passed *nem con*. Claudius has managed to square the circle of "mirth in funeral" and "dirge in marriage" without a murmur. The calmness with which the status quo is adumbrated contrasts interestingly, for example, with that of King Lear's tyrannising in that play's expository scene – which has already begun to run into bad-tempered opposition before the scene is out. Here, the court – Hamlet apart – has evidently acquiesced in a catalogue of bad acts without demur. The most outrageous of these is Claudius's marriage, an incestuous affair as it surely was in those times and for long afterwards. The speed of this second marriage after Hamlet senior's death ("A little month" as we are to learn) is another offence to decency. Claudius negotiates it in a speech of prolix hypocrisy. In his study *An Approach to Hamlet* (1960) L.C.

Knights acutely compares Claudius's performance here with "the tone and accent of Milton's Belial" as he addresses the infernal council with a speech "clothed in reason's garb" in Book II of *Paradise Lost*. The "ignoble ease and peaceful sloth" which Milton deplores in Belial (in marked contrast to the vigour of Satan which he cannot help making attractive) are the hallmarks, too, of Claudius's court. And the "better wisdoms" of the members of the council that has ratified the king's marriage are simply corrupt. "Something is rotten in the state of Denmark", as Marcellus is later to observe (Act I, scene 4, 90). Just how comprehensively rotten, neither he, nor even Hamlet, can, at that stage, have any notion.

In his absorbing chapter on *Hamlet* in his book *Form and Meaning in Drama* (1956) the classical scholar H.D.F. Kitto suggests that we try to see the play in terms of the religious drama of the Greeks. This is as far as can be from suggesting a Christian, ecclesiastical approach to it. In classical Greek literature, as Kitto points out: "There is religious drama in which gods do not appear, and secular drama in which they do." He merely asks us to consider the universe of *Hamlet* in the same light as that in which the protagonists of a drama by Sophocles operate, a place where there exists, as there does for Hamlet, "a divinity that shapes our ends" (Act V, scene 2, 10). This does not imply an inescapable predestination (as it does, for example, for Sophocles's Oedipus) but something akin to what was understood in that pact which the Greeks acknowledged as existing between men and the gods – that, at the end, evil acts will meet with retribution. In Elsinore, Kitto argues, Hamlet is not confronted by one, or even several evils – the murder of his father; his mother's apostasy; his loss of the throne – serious though these are, but by evil itself. Kitto's approach, it seems to me, immediately allows us to bring to what has happened, and what will happen, in *Hamlet*, a level of seriousness that so much commentary misses. Hamlet's predicament ceases to be merely his personal problem, vengeance – just though that cause is. And our approach to the play is liberated from the mere consideration of the effectiveness, or otherwise, of his performance of that. Evil has been unleashed in Elsinore, and, being what and who he is, Hamlet is drawn inexorably to the centre of the struggle against it.

For the moment, a good deal of this is invisible to him. Most importantly, he is ignorant of the mode of his father's death. But he sees enough to perceive that the world of Elsinore has become "an unweeded garden/That grows to seed" (Act I, scene 2, 135-6). Denmark is now possessed by "things rank and gross", and these are exemplified by his mother's betrayal, against which Hamlet's nature is in a revolt expressed in the most pointed disgust:

A little month, or e'er those shoes were old
With which she followed my poor father's body
Like Niobe, all tears, why she, even she –
O God, a beast that wants discourse of reason
Would have mourned longer –
(Act 1, scene 2, 147-51)

This is strong stuff from a son on his mother. Yet to him she has sunk to become something lower than bestial. The vileness of her act has tainted him, too. He can scarcely bear to be confronted with it daily. But there is to be no escape from it either by the spontaneous dissolution of his body for which he so ardently wishes at the beginning of this great soliloquy ("O that this too too sullied flesh would melt") – which, alas, will not happen – or through recourse to a suicide that is forbidden by God's edict.

The brooding, almost unendurable anguish of Hamlet's mind is galvanised as soon as the council is broken up and Horatio and Marcellus enter with the news of his father. There is something more utterly riveting in Horatio's simple assertion "My lord, I think I saw him yesternight" (Act I, scene 2, 189) than the simple words can, in themselves, well convey. Their dramatic charge is something to do with the light they suddenly shine into a dark place. Until this point, the justice of his feelings notwithstanding, Hamlet has cut a poor figure in Elsinore. What he is not to know is that his mental faculties are being systematically abused by Claudius. He can sense wrongdoing but, given the acquiescence of the king's council, has been in no position to identify the source of his unease. The miasma of the court that has hung over his spirits is suddenly dispelled and he is a host of eager demands: "Saw? Who?", "The King my father?", "For God's love, let me hear!" (Act I, scene 2, 190, 191, 196).

As Hamlet drinks in the details of their recital of what they have seen, the earlier introspection, and the truculence to his own mother, as well as to Claudius, dissipate. He has at last been presented with a key to unlock his perceptions of the Elsinore he has been living in since his father's death and mother's marriage.

> My father's spirit! In arms! All is not well.
> I doubt [= fear] some foul play. Would the night were
>   come!
> Till then sit still, my soul. Foul deeds will rise,
> Though all the earth o'erwhelm them, to men's eyes.
>
> (Act I, scene 2, 255-8)

His dimly felt presentiments of some wrongdoing have suddenly taken a more concrete form. His mind is invigorated. He nerves himself to rise to the level of events, whatever they may be, and to a confrontation with the Ghost. Of this he is not in the slightest bit afraid.

From these fearsome mental crags we are brought down to the domestic tone of the opening of the next scene. Laertes is ready to sail for France, and he takes leave of his sister Ophelia and his father. It is apparently all geniality and family affection. 'Good old' Polonius has been commended so often by critics down the ages for his homely wisdom. Where he has been granted to have shortcomings they have been thought of only as a tendency to meddle and allow himself to become the butt of jokes.

Yet the sunny surface of scene 3 seems to me to mask a mentality no less corrupt than that of Claudius. Polonius's words to Laertes: "This above all: to thine own self be true/...Thou canst not then be false to any man", (Act I, scene 3, 78) have been quoted so often (generally out of context) and, indeed, so frequently been proffered as advice to their children by parents who have never read *Hamlet*, that it seems almost a hopeless task, now, to object that taken in context they are not wisdom, but worldly wisdom, and that taken out of context they are meaningless. To address the latter case first: were not Hitler and his Nazi thugs utterly true to themselves in what they thought and what they did? As for Polonius and his advice to his son, it comes at the end of a catalogue of maxims on such banal matters as dress, manners, personal conduct and personal spending. It is at best humdrum, and at worst in a contemptible vein of worldly caution in the conduct of personal life. It has more in common with the worldly advice (so pithily deplored by Dr Johnson) to be found in the letters of the 18th-century politician and diplomat, the 4th Earl of Chesterfield, to his son, than with attaining *sprezzatura* – that carelessly-worn, effortless superiority that was so admired by the Renaissance. But in this scene Polonius shows his real rottenness in his advice to Ophelia on her confession of her attachment to Hamlet. He sneers at her from the outset "Pooh! You speak like a green girl,/Unsifted in such perilous circumstance." (Act I, scene 3, 101-2). There is something particularly vile in the way he twists her words:

> My lord he hath importuned me with love
> In honourable fashion
>
> (Act I, scene 3, 110-11)

to give them a disreputable meaning. It is quite evident that by "fashion" she means simply 'manner'. He chooses to throw it back in her face as implying some sort of flirtatious style of fashionable wooing, something that would not be, from Hamlet's standpoint, as Polonius sees it, remotely to be taken seriously. (Significantly, her brother, whom we shall later see to be as corruptible as his father, has already put this construction on Hamlet's interest in her – and told her as much.) Polonius goes on to brush aside Ophelia's assurances in language that besmirches both Hamlet's affection and her estimate of it.

> Do not believe his vows. For they are brokers,
> Not of that dye which their investments show,
> But mere implorators of unholy suits,
> Breathing like sanctified and pious bawds,
> The better to beguile.
>
> (Act I, scene 3, 127-31)

This is a young girl (but not, as we shall see, a weak-minded one) in the innocent enjoyment of her first love. Her suitor is the heir to the throne and she is, perhaps, the second lady in the land. (We have no other candidates in view among the dramatis personae.) She is certainly not someone beneath Hamlet's serious consideration. And her father's reaction is: 'Don't be a fool. Don't make me a fool. Don't believe him. Everything he says is simply to seduce you.' And the language in which he berates her is shot through with the suggestive imagery of go-betweens, pimps and commercial sex. A corrupt man himself, Polonius can only think corruptly of the motives of others.

What is doubly diabolical here, of course, is that when he accounts to Claudius and Gertrude for his advice to Ophelia on Hamlet's courting, he tells them an outright lie. Has he encouraged his daughter in any way?

> No, I went round to work,
> And my young mistress thus did I bespeak:
> 'Lord Hamlet is a prince, out of thy star.
> This must not be.'
>
> (Act II, scene 2, 139-42)

There are two things that strike our notice, here. Firstly, the king had not thought it important to ask Polonius what his advice to Ophelia was in the first place, but merely asked, disinterestedly, and in the context of Hamlet's sudden madness: "But how hath she/ Received his love?" (Act II, scene 2, 128-9). And the second is that not only is the substance of what Polonius says false – he nowhere mentions Ophelia's ineligibility, if ineligibility it is, to her – but the friendly tone of the exchange with Ophelia that he suggests, is also a lie.

It is important to be clear, I think, that Polonius's lies are not harmless things. And it is wrong to represent him on stage as, at worst, a lovable old fool. His falsehoods and deviousness are insidious and destructive to all they touch. Even Claudius is bamboozled by him. When at Act II, scene 2, 153, Polonius challenges him: "Hath there been such a time – I would fain know that –/that I have positively said ''Tis so'/When it hath proved otherwise?" the King concedes (albeit grudgingly?): "Not that I know." The result of this admission is Claudius's acquiescence in the disastrous plan to spy on Hamlet and Ophelia in Act III. And the upshot is that Claudius comes (erroneously) to the conclusion that his only safety is Hamlet's dispatch to a death in England. It is ultimately to cost his creatures Rosencrantz and Guildenstern their lives, and bring Hamlet back to Denmark to be his nemesis.

We next witness Polonius acting to besmirch the reputation of the very son whom he has just seen off on his way to Paris with a hatful of wholesome advice. In the truly fantastic performance of Act II scene 1 we see him 'briefing' his man Reynaldo to spread slanders against Laertes among his Danish acquaintains in the city. This is not a scene with which Shakespeare has been merely saddled from an earlier version of the play. He devotes far too much craft to it – far too much palpable enjoyment of its content – for its effect to be accidental.

Having been asked to take Laertes some more funds and "make inquire" of his behaviour – a proposition he evidently does not much take to – Reynaldo is made increasingly uneasy at the drift of Polonius's proposals:

> POLONIUS
> Inquire me first what Danskers are in Paris,
> And how, and who, what means, and where they keep,
> What company, at what expense; and finding
> By this encompassment and drift of question
> That they do know my son, come you more nearer
> Than your particular demands will touch it.
> Take you as 'twere some distant knowledge of him,
> As thus, 'I know his father and his friends,
> And in part him' – do you mark this, Reynaldo?
>
> (Act II, scene 1, 7-15)

The way his instructions are put creates the same moral haze around the proposed transaction as we were aware of in Claudius's earlier peroration to his court. Reynaldo's reply, a wary: "Ay, very well", by no means satisfies this dysfunctional father, who having already attempted to pollute the mind of his daughter, has not yet finished with his son, either.

> POLONIUS
> 'And in part him, but,' you may say, 'not well;
> But if 't be he I mean, he's very wild,
> Addicted so and so.' And there put on him
> What forgeries you please – marry, none so rank
> As may dishonour him – take heed of that –
> But, sir, such wanton, wild, and usual slips

As are companions noted and most known
To youth and liberty.

(Act II, scene 1, 17-24)

By now, Reynaldo, thoroughly uneasy, feels obliged to advance some modest proposition of his own, if only to show willing. But his tentative "As gaming, my lord" will not at all do for Polonius whose mind is hot in the imagination of a whole catalogue of vices: "Ay, or drinking, fencing, swearing, quarrelling,/Drabbing. You may go so far."

There is something truly pathological about Polonius's sordid interest in the sexual lives of his children. In the previous act Hamlet's "tenders … of affection", as Ophelia described them, had become the "implorators of unholy suits" within an instant of their being acquired by the antennae of his unwholesome sensibility. His instinctive assumption about the sexual career of Laertes is that it will include "drabbing", i.e. frequenting prostitutes. Now, using 'drabs', i.e. common prostitutes, may have been a natural outlet for the sex drive of a young man of Laertes's rank in life, but one would imagine not. (He would undoubtedly have gained sexual experience through the freedom of manners available to him in ladies of somewhat higher station.) Reynaldo, though he has presumably been in Polonius's household for some years, certainly does not think it is, and he doubly recoils from the idea that he should be the instrument of the slander: "My lord, that would dishonour him."

By now, Reynaldo is thoroughly appalled by what is expected of him. Polonius is, like much else in King Claudius's Denmark, rotten to the core. Unlike Claudius, whom we see in at least one moment of conscience, he is completely unaware of just how rotten he is.

The last two scenes of Act I returned us to the bracing air of the battlements. There, Hamlet is to learn the facts of his father's death. Interestingly, Shakespeare does not cut immediately to the entrance of the Ghost. Instead we are reminded again of the state of affairs in Denmark. And Shakespeare introduces this in a way that is calculated to be striking. Even amid the tension of anticipation of the Ghost's entry we cannot fail to notice it.

The stage direction: *A flourish of trumpets, and two pieces of ordnance go off*, is followed by Horatio's startled inquiry "What does this mean, my lord?" (Act I, scene 4, 7). As we saw in the first

18

battlements scene, Shakespeare does not contrive such effects for no reason. The cannons, we learn, are yet another instance of the degeneration of the body politic. There is nothing martial about their being fired in this context. Rather:

> The king doth wake tonight and takes his rouse,
> Keeps wassail, and the swaggering upspring reels.
> And as he drains his draughts of Rhenish down
> The kettledrum and trumpet thus bray out
> The triumph of his pledge.
>
> (Act I, scene 4, 8-12)

The king drinks nightly, and for every draught that goes down the gunpowder for two cannon salutes is expended. Such is the military economy of a country that is apparently nervously preparing for some threat to its security. And worse, this propensity is widely known by other nations, who "clepe us drunkards and with swinish phrase/ Soil our addition" (Act I, scene 4, 19-20). Interestingly, this puerile predilection for punctuating his wassails with cannon fire remains with Claudius right to the end of the play. It surfaces again during Hamlet's fencing bout with Laertes and, I think, not incidentally. Having scored a hit on Laertes, Hamlet is invited to join Claudius in a toast as the cannons fire from the battlements above. Hamlet will brook no such frivolity. Swordplay – even as an exercise – is far too serious a business to mix with the consumption of alcohol. The distant echo of Hamlet's disapproval in Act I is immediately striking.

The entry of the Ghost and the beginning of his explanation come to Hamlet both as a kind of relief and a self-justification. To the revelation that "The serpent that did sting thy father's life/Now wears his crown" (Act I, scene 5, 38-9), his reaction is not, for the moment, at least, shock or disbelief but "O my prophetic soul!" The corrupting miasma of the court, which had lain heavily on his soul, slips off. And by the time the Ghost has concluded his tale, the undermining unease and dislike he had felt in relation to his mother and stepfather have been replaced with a cleansing moral revulsion. They have become respectively "O most pernicious woman!/O villain, villain, smiling, damnèd villain!" (Act I, scene 5, 105-6). It is not great poetry, but as high abuse it effectively expresses the sense of a purging of the canker of months of doubt. Unless the Ghost is, indeed, as he had first wondered, a "goblin damned", Hamlet is as last in possession of the *fons et origo* of the deep-seated malady that afflicts Denmark's life.

A much debated question is left hanging in the air at the end of Act I: was Gertrude having an affair with Claudius before he killed old Hamlet? If she was then it seems impossible to imagine that she was unaware that there was some foul play in her first husband's death, and that Claudius had ambitions for the throne. Pillow talk would surely in the end have at least touched on these possibilities. Given that, it seems doubly impossible, too, that she should be able to bear herself so utterly guiltlessly in her role as Queen of Denmark for the second time round. For that is what she does. She could not/ would not, for example, say to her second husband in private when there is no earthly chance of a third party's hearing them, that the cause of her son's madness is "no other but the main,/His father's death and our o'erhasty marriage" (Act II, scene 2, 56-7). Claudius, too, never treats her as the woman with whom he has shared the guilty pleasure of enjoying her as a mistress. He addresses her at all times with respect and treats her as an honoured wife. It is one of the few honest aspects of his life.

Admittedly, the Ghost does describe his murderer to Hamlet as "that incestuous, that adulterate beast", (Act I, scene 5, 42) and he goes on to deprecate the fact that Claudius "won to his shameful lust/The will of my most seeming-virtuous Queen" (Act I, scene 5, 45-6). Some critics have, I think rightly, seen this as being a merely figurative usage. The Ghost is, after all, in a state of intemperate indignation, and under pressure of that is allowing himself to exaggerate – as in our own times a cuckolded husband might easily be driven under the pressure of humiliation to describing his wife to third parties as a 'whore' without in the slightest meaning to suggest that she is actually a prostitute.

That assumption has been challenged by John Dover Wilson in his influential study *What Happens in Hamlet* (1935). He asks "Why then should the Ghost waste precious moments telling Hamlet what he was fully cognisant of before?" – i.e. Claudius's successful wooing of Gertrude to be his wife *after* her first husband's death. There is something in the viewpoint, and yet Hamlet senior would hardly think to express his sense of his wife's (adulterous) betrayal to his son in terms of "O Hamlet, what a falling off was there,/From me .../Upon a wretch whose natural gifts were poor/To those of mine" (Act I, scene 5, 47-52).The adultery itself would be the act to be deplored, not the fact that Gertrude had 'done it' with someone whom old Hamlet felt to be poor stuff. It seems to me that this must mean: 'After so long living with a splendid chap like me, how on earth could she have married *him*?'

On a later occasion (Act V, scene 2, 64) Hamlet himself is to describe the sequence of fault thus: "He that hath killed my King and whored my mother." The overriding impression, right at the end of the play, is that he sees Gertrude's second marriage not as part of the criminal act that has removed his father, but merely as an utterly reprehensible consequence of it. In neither the dumb show nor the Gonzago play in which Hamlet confronts Claudius with his crime, is adultery *before* the murder, suggested. Yet if Hamlet had really wanted to have Claudius – and his mother – 'bang to rights' with the facts as he understood them from the Ghost, it surely would have been.

As for Gertrude, as she watches Hamlet's entertainment, her commentary on the play queen's assurances of fidelity to her first husband: "The lady doth protest too much, methinks" (Act III, scene 2, 240) seems to me to acquit her of any knowledge of Claudius's crime. And when, shortly after the play Hamlet goes to her chamber and violently confronts her, we are, surely, to take her innocent reaction, "What have I done that thou darest wag thy tongue/In noise so rude against me?" (Act III, scene 4, 40-1) at face value. Gertrude has many reprehensible faults, but they tend to stem from (an admittedly considerable) moral laziness. She nowhere exhibits the ruthless scheming and hypocrisy – the sheer wickedness – that would be required to brazen out the secret of old Hamlet's murder without at some point betraying herself.

3

Hamlet and Ophelia

Ophelia has not, as a character, fared well on the page or at the hands of the critics. In his excellent introduction to the Arden edition of the play, Harold Jenkins laments that "it is not too much to say that the failure to get Ophelia right has frustrated the interpretation of the tragedy". While in relation to Ophelia and Hamlet's love for her, A.C. Bradley confessed (*Shakespearean Tragedy*) "I am unable to arrive at a conviction as to the meaning of some of his words and deeds, and I question whether from the mere text of the play a sure interpretation of them can be drawn." For Dover Wilson "The attitude of Hamlet towards Ophelia is without doubt the greatest of all the puzzles in the play."

These critical uncertainties have not stopped Ophelia from having her moments in the theatre, since women first appeared on the stage with the Restoration in 1660. There she has progressed from the literally and spectacularly love-maddened Susan Mountfort of a Lincoln's Inn Fields production of 1720, via the stately, classical Sarah Siddons of 1785, to the beginning of the Romantic style, inaugurated in Paris by Harriet Smithson with Kemble's troupe in 1827. Smithson's impassioned performance, imbued with the sexual mystery of the Gothic novel, so entranced the composer Hector Berlioz, who was in the audience, that he married her in spite of the vehement opposition of his father.

The Romantic interpretation of the part, with its protagonist depicted as being driven mad by love, held sway in the theatre from that moment, until well after the Second World War. One of its most remarkable exponents was the great Ellen Terry, who visited lunatic asylums to study models for emulation in the mad scene – but found their inmates "too theatrical" to learn from.

Approaches to the role from the 1970s onwards have scouted the idea of a sexual attraction between Ophelia and Laertes (Helen Mirren, Marianne Faithfull and Yvonne Nicholson), while more recent studies have seen the role in terms of a mental illness such as schizophrenia, thus usurping the notion of female possession by erotomania which so fascinated the (male) 17th century, with its conviction that women were constitutionally unchaste. Feminist readings of the role have also had their say, quintessentially expressed in such a play as Melissa Murray's 1979 propagandist version *Ophelia*, for the women's theatre group Hormone Imbalance, in which the protagonist discovers her true lesbian self, and runs away to join a guerrilla commune.

But these interpretations have tended to hold audiences either by ingenious, provoking or 'shock' direction or, in the case of 19th-century productions, through riveting, atmospheric performances from great actresses, which achieved their effect often with scant reference to Shakespeare's text. This question of the apparently 'lost cause' of Ophelia's lines on the page has dogged the efforts of generations of critics understandably unwilling to write off completely her importance to the scheme of the play.

In this process, analysis of Ophelia has nevertheless been partly hampered by a lingering paternalistic view of her character and capacities. Thus, the normally hard-headed Dover Wilson (*What Happens in Hamlet*) finds himself in sentimental Victorian mode in characterising her, in the face of Hamlet's "coarse" language to her (of which more anon), as a "gentle and inoffensive child". While more recently the influential American feminist critic Elaine Showalter in her essay "Representing Ophelia" (*Shakespeare and the Question of Theory*, ed. Patricia Barker & Geoffrey Hartman, 1985) complains that "Shakespeare gives us very little information from which to imagine a past for Ophelia," and dismisses her brusquely as "a creature of lack".

Yet when we first come across Ophelia, is she really such a pallid character as this? We are lucky enough to catch her, not among her elders in court, nor with her father, but in a situation best calculated to bring out her nature free from constraint. She is alone with her brother who is about to leave Elsinore for his journey back to Paris, and the atmosphere is one of affectionate farewell. Laertes's tone is that of an elder brother, just slightly hectoring as he insists "do not sleep/ But let me hear from you". (Act I, scene 3, 3-4). Her answer is very far from being in the mode of 'Oh yes, of course dear brother' but is dignified: "Do you doubt that?" It is quite obvious that she has always been a good correspondent, and while there is no element of reproach in her response, she is not going to let him get away with suggesting otherwise.

The subject of her relations with Hamlet has obviously come up between them. He – as his father is shortly to do – assumes the worst of Hamlet's interest in her. There is prurience in his admonition that goes well beyond the good natured 'take it easy' which is surely the very most that is required here.

> Then weigh what loss your honour may sustain
> If with too credent ear you list his songs,
> Or lose your heart, or your chaste treasure open
> To his unmastered importunity.
> Fear it, Ophelia, fear it, my dear sister.
>
> (Act I, scene 3, 29-33)

It might be added to the list of corrupting attributes of the Danish court that Laertes, whom Hamlet later generously styles "a noble youth", is unwilling to ascribe a scrap of decency to the throne of Denmark's heir. But for the moment that is not important. What is, is Ophelia's civil, but firm rebuke to her brother's gratuitous advice.

> I shall the effect of this good lesson keep
> As watchman to my heart. But, good my brother,
> Do not, as some ungracious pastors do,
> Show me the steep and thorny way to heaven
> Whiles like a puffed and reckless libertine
> Himself the primrose path of dalliance treads
> And recks not his own rede.
>
> (Act I, scene 3, 45-51)

This is quite unequivocal as a comment on Ophelia's perception and intelligence (and of her knowledge of the world?). It is surely the utterance of someone of considerable strength of character – and, we might observe, low tolerance of hypocrisy.

We are, of course, fated never to witness the love of Hamlet and

Ophelia 'in action'. It is already a thing of the past by the time we see them together, a victim of her father's ban on it. All we know about it, as she subsequently defends herself from dirty-minded insinuations from Polonius, is that she believes herself to be the fortunate object of Hamlet's honourable approaches. From what we have seen to this point, we would back her judgment against that of Laertes or her father.

It is, of course, simply not available to her to make the saucy riposte she has just made to Laertes, to Polonius when he speaks of her love for Hamlet in similar (or, as we have already seen, even more disreputable) terms. He is her father, and his unequivocal injunction to end the relationship puts the matter beyond further discussion. Her inescapable duty of obedience to a man of such wickedness and folly is her personal tragedy. The promise of a happy love is blighted. The twin blows of this, and the death of her father at Hamlet's hands are to destroy her mind.

The effect of her father's order to break off with Hamlet is very soon apparent. Her reaction to it says a good deal about her character. Her report to Polonius of Hamlet's coming to her closet is a thing of great vividness. Remarkably, it is completely devoid of self-pity. Her imagination is directed wholly towards the man she thinks she has wronged. And even in her distress, in her interpretation of Hamlet's frame of mind: "As if he had been loosèd out of hell/ To speak of horrors – he comes before me" (Act II, scene 1, 83-4) she has actually hit upon the truth. For, since the revelations of the Ghost, hell is exactly the mental terrain Hamlet has, in part, been inhabiting. She is not to know that his appearance to her, "Pale as his shirt, his knees knocking each other" is part of the "antic disposition" he has decided to put on since these revelations. Nor is she to know that Hamlet's subsequent bitterness against her is not merely the resentment of a jilted man, but is part of a great sickness of heart that she, and what she stands for in his estimation, appear now to have become one with the general corruption that afflicts the Danish court.

In his 1934 edition of the play for the Cambridge University Press, Dover Wilson moved Hamlet's entry in Act II scene 2, in which the King and Polonius arrange to hide and overhear his later confrontation with Ophelia from line 167 (Penguin text) to some ten lines earlier.

This alteration, ingeniously argued in Dover Wilson's introduction to the play, and backed up in *What Happens in Hamlet*, has much to recommend it from a director's point of view.

Hamlet now becomes an eavesdropper on the details of the plot as it is discussed. He knows that his encounter with Ophelia (which is to take place in Act III, scene 1) will not be a chance one. She will have been "loosed" to him courtesy of Polonius, as a horse breeder might loose a mare to a stallion, or a farmer a cow to a bull, to be mated. Hamlet thus knows that Claudius and Polonius are hiding behind the arras, and that Ophelia is an accomplice in their stratagem to elicit the truth of his madness from him. It, of course, makes Hamlet's reactions, most specifically his verbal violence towards Ophelia, easier to understand for an audience. It also creates an opportunity for a good deal of menacing stage business as he harangues Ophelia and 'plays to the gallery' of the two men hidden behind the arras, and enables him to threaten the King, directly.

But at the same time it trivialises the psychological depth of the scene. It turns Hamlet's profound agony of spirit at the conviction that Ophelia has, of her own volition, become part of Elsinore's corrupt heart, into the mere petulant anger of a jilted lover. It makes something truly dramatic merely theatrical. It diminishes to mere caprice the impact of those terrible words with which he answers her cruelly misguided, mistimed, attempt to return his gifts:

> OPHELIA
> My lord, I have remembrances of yours
> That I have longèd long to re-deliver.
> I pray you now receive them.
> HAMLET
> No, not I.
> I never gave you aught
>
> (Act III, scene 1, 93-6)

Of course he does not mean merely that he did not give her tokens of his love, or that if he did, they were not intended in good faith. It is an anguished attempt, from a man, now profoundly disillusioned, to deny that he ever shared any part of himself with her. Here is a man who has prostrated his being before a woman he truly loved. *Doubt truth to be a liar./But never doubt I love* runs the love note that Polonius and the King (Act II, scene 2, 117-8) impudently pollute with their jocularity after the former has extorted it from his daughter to be used as evidence. He now, apparently, finds it flung in his face. He has no idea, of course, that she is acting under orders from her father.

And yet, here we have two high-minded young people who are in reality still desperately in love. Like Ophelia, Hamlet is suffering acutely. If Shakespeare had really intended Hamlet to have overheard the Polonius/Claudius plot, as Dover Wilson insists, and for him therefore to be forewarned of Ophelia's complicity in their designs, he could never have had him say, as he does when he suddenly realises he is in her presence, walking alone:

> Soft you now,
> The fair Ophelia! – Nymph, in thy orisons
> Be all my sins remembered.
>
> (Act III, scene 1, 88-90)

His tone is not just one of exalted feeling and love, but of respect and admiration. She is the one person in this hellhole whose prayers for him might have some redemptive power. But she spoils it. In thrall to the plot cooked up between Polonius and the King, she approaches him, inappropriately asking him to take back his gifts.

Rebuffed with "I never gave you aught", she nevertheless keeps on trying. The injunction of her father behind the arras is completely forgotten in remembrances that powerfully rekindle her love.

> My honoured lord, you know right well you did,
> And with them words of so sweet breath composed
> As made the things more rich.
>
> (Act III, scene 1, 97-9)

It is too late. In his despair Hamlet increasingly retreats to the refuge of the antic disposition, with its inverted aperçus and wranglings, that has served him so well. " … if you be honest and fair, your honesty should admit no discourse to your beauty." Catching at his vein of wit, she battles desperately on, defending herself and her status as a woman: "Could beauty, my lord, have better commerce than with honesty?" Flashes of consciousness of what they have shared momentarily surface gasping from the abyss of revulsion that grips Hamlet's mind. "I did love you once", "Indeed, my lord, you made me believe so". But these brief moments cannot endure the weight of Hamlet's bitterness. This is not play acting. "Get thee to a nunnery," he snarls at her, "Why wouldst thou be a breeder of sinners?" (Act III, scene 1, 121-2) The vileness of his mother's misdeed torments him afresh, and takes him to the anguished verges of reason. Ophelia is mown down in the articulate torrent of a cynicism that comprehends all women, and of which she is at that moment, alas for her, the only visible symbol.

He flings away with the final injunction: "To a nunnery, go." (Act III, scene 1, 150). And the sobbing girl is left with her blasted hopes and anguished reflections. Remarkably, there is in them no tinct of self-pity. Her thoughts are only for what Hamlet was, and what, in her perception, he has now become.

> O, what a noble mind is here o'erthrown!
> The courtier's, soldier's, scholar's, eye, tongue, sword,
> Th'expectancy and rose of the fair state,
> The glass of fashion and the mould of form,
> Th'observed of all observers, quite, quite down!
> (Act III, scene 1, 151-5)

Quite apart from the light they throw on the quality of Ophelia's mental equipment (they are hardly the musings of a silly girl, nor, surely of "a disreputable young woman": Rebecca West, *The Court and the Castle*, 1957), these lines are a compelling description of Hamlet as the exemplar of renaissance princely virtues. Master though he is at creating character through action and dialogue, it is Shakespeare's habit, at times, to step back and furnish us with a 'character reference', as it were, of his protagonist, from the mouth of a third party. And what better witness to that character than a woman of sensibility whose love is deep but so clear sighted? For it is not the loss of Hamlet's money, his good looks, his rank in society, or his sporting prowess that Ophelia laments here, but the collapse of his intellect:

> … that noble and most sovereign reason
> Like sweet bells jangled, out of time and harsh,
> (Act III, scene 1, 158-9)

Surely, this love, if any in Shakespeare does, qualifies as the "marriage of true minds" that was his ideal of the mature basis for an enduring relationship between man and woman. Its destruction is Polonius's achievement. For Hamlet and Ophelia there is to be no road back from this. There is, however, to be a further encounter between them, and it is one of Hamlet's choosing. Critics have been virtually unanimous in their condemnation of the 'coarseness' of Hamlet's language to her in the play scene. For Bradley (*Shakespearean Tragedy*), it is "disgusting and insulting", "such language as you will find addressed to no other woman by a hero of Shakespeare's". Dover Wilson deplored it as "savagery towards a gentle and inoffensive child".

I am not certain about this. As that astute and knowledgeable man of the theatre, Harley Granville-Barker, concedes (*Prefaces to Shakespeare*, 1937), "There was freedom of speech enough in Renaissance Courts." Though he goes on to retreat to the position that Ophelia is "very young … and the thing is an insult". But we only have to look at the candid language of the Tudor madrigal to get a flavour of how free exchange of sentiment was among members of the opposite sex in those times, and not just in the society of the court. The members of mixed parties of young singers in large family houses must have smiled to each other as they sang of pastoral sexual activity in the part songs of such composers as Dowland and Wilbye, with their frequent references to "dying" (orgasm).

In others of his plays, Shakespeare's purest heroines listen to, and apparently enjoy, trading sexual badinage with men. In *Othello* Desdemona is, it seems, quite at home, while she anxiously awaits the arrival of her husband, in an extended passage of crude backchat with Iago and Cassio (Act II, scene 1). While in *The Merchant of Venice* Portia at times takes the lead in schemes of brazenness. Indeed, the play's very last scene concludes with a crude double entendre involving her maid Nerissa's wedding ring and her encircling vagina (Act V, scene 1).

And how young would a young woman of the period have to be to need protection from sexual innuendo? Nothing like as old as the middle-class girl of eighteen or nineteen that the Edwardian Bradley envisages. In *Romeo and Juliet* Shakespeare has his fourteen-year-old heroine complaining that she is "sold/But not enjoyed," as she eagerly contemplates the forthcoming sexual activity of her wedding night. In Ophelia's case, a girl who has heard her attachment to Hamlet described by her own father in terms of the commercial trade in sex, who has been told by her brother that she is an object merely for seduction, is hardly likely to blush at sexual terminology *per se*. In her later 'madness' Ophelia's own language, too, is shot through with a realistic understanding of what sexual relations are, and how badly a young woman is likely to come out of them if she is left to a man's mercy. Even a madwoman cannot give utterance to things she knows nothing about.

The more interesting question, as Hamlet, on edge in Act III, scene 2 as he prepares for the play which he hopes will confirm the Ghost's veracity, and 'out' Claudius as his father's murderer, is: why at that moment does he single out the young woman he had apparently so definitively turned his back on in the previous scene? The answer is probably a rather simple one, but none the less unfortunate for that, from Ophelia's point of view.

Who knows where Hamlet might have decided to sit in the audience on that evening, if left to his own devices? But as he walks into the hall where the court is assembling for the night's entertainment, his mother fondly appropriates him to her: "Come hither, my dear Hamlet, sit by me" (Act III, scene 2, 118). This is the last thing he wants, either from the point of observing Claudius's reaction to what is to take place on stage, or from his very strong feelings that he does not want to be petted by the woman who has so rankly betrayed his father.

The recourse to Ophelia, "No, good mother. Here's metal more attractive", may be simply a displacement reaction, though we would like to think that is part of a deep attraction to her, which he still cannot resist. It is to be the beginning of a miserable night for her. "Lady, shall I lie in your lap?" he asks, the proposition here carrying obvious sexual innuendo, in which sense, preposterous as such a manner of address seems in such circumstances, even to our moral latitude, it is instinctively accepted by her, since she ripostes firmly, and without any sense of wanting to share in the jest, "No, my lord". He pretends that he had only meant "my head upon your lap", in which proposition she wretchedly acquiesces. Again, this proposal of intimacy is pretty remarkable, given what has passed between them.

We can feel that the stuffing has been knocked out of her since her passionate last-ditch attempt to engage his affections at their last encounter. To his next piece of ribaldry: "Do you think I meant country matters?" (i.e. sexual intercourse), she can only mutter that she thinks "nothing". To this he immediately attaches the word's sexual construction ("That's a fair thought – to lie between maids' legs") – "nothing" being a term in Elizabethan times for signifying the female genitalia, represented as they were (in polite art at any rate) as a smooth, hairless absence of visual interest, on which the painter could lavish no realistic detail, nothing suitable for public consumption, at any rate.

Even if we acquit Hamlet's language here of indecency, it does him no credit, as a way of talking to a young woman of whom he has been an admirer. Yet she seems puzzled, wearied perhaps, rather than affronted. For there has become something impersonal about his sallies of wit, here. He is in a state of high tension over the success or failure of his dramatic experiment this evening. This kind of wit comes all too naturally to him, and, alas, Ophelia just happens to be the butt of it. When reminded, as he looks across at her, of his mother's betrayal of his father, it takes a more caustic turn in bitterness, a bitterness that has nothing to do specifically with Ophelia, though she is willy-nilly in the line of fire here.

> O God, your only jig-maker! What should a man do but be
> merry? For look you how cheerfully my mother looks, and
> my father died within's two hours.
>
> (Act III, scene 2, 134-6)

Fatally for her (is it something to do, as some critics have observed, that in her new role as "ex" she is bound to reply with conventional platitudes to the man who now reverts from being suitor, to "lord"?) she replies somewhat stuffily: "Nay, 'tis twice two months, my lord." Which draws the tart riposte:

> So long? Nay then, let the devil wear black, for I'll have a
> suit of sables. O heavens! Die two months ago, and not
> forgotten yet? Then there's hope a great man's memory
> may outlive his life half a year.
>
> (Act III, scene 2, 138-41)

31

Yet there is agony close beneath this cynical wit. To give his riposte a more dramatic point, Hamlet has contracted her "twice two months" to "two months". We are more likely to prefer her memory on the point to his. It does not really matter, except, perhaps, to remind us, as T.J.B. Spencer, editor of the Penguin edition, points out, that a good deal more than two months has elapsed since the Ghost's injunction to Hamlet, if we consider that at the opening of the play we are given the impression that his mother's marriage, contracted a month after his father's death, is a quite recent affair. In that time he has failed to act on it.

We shall not see much more of the 'sane' Ophelia. From the point the players' performance opens, Hamlet's replies to what little she says are increasingly abstracted. He is in a state of painful anxiety that the actors shall not 'muck up' his production, specifically the speech of his own composition that he has had inserted in it, to increase its relevance to the circumstances of his father's murder. And I think Spencer is right to point out that his riposte, "As woman's love", to Ophelia's comment on the play's prologue, " 'Tis brief, my lord" (Act III, scene 2, 162) is not as heartless as it appears at face value. By that point, on the verge of the stage performance that is to portray his uncle's crime and his mother's faithlessness, he is thinking in this remark not of Ophelia, but of Gertrude.

But for a few more ribaldries, flung off tangentially as the play gets under way and the tension within him mounts, this is the last we shall see of Hamlet and Ophelia. He is out of the way, overseas, at the last scene of her life, and she must die without him. It is only after her death that his love for her is again expressed.

In the meantime, what are we to make of her 'madness'? Of course the 'burden of evidence', so to speak, that a drama would today need to furnish of some mental illness or psychotic condition to make such a scene convincing, is not necessary here. For Shakespeare, and indeed for authors for hundreds of years after him, people were simply allowed to go 'mad' in conditions of intolerable grief or stress. But is there anything specific to be read into Ophelia's losing her wits? What has caused it? Hamlet's cruelty? Her father's death? Or a combination of both?

For the psychiatrist R.D. Laing (*The Divided Self*, 1959) Shakespeare *does* in fact furnish evidence enough to satisfy the modern palate. For him, the verdict on Ophelia is unequivocal: "Clinically she is latterly undoubtedly a schizophrenic. In her madness, there is no one there. She is not a person. There is no integral selfhood expressed through her actions or utterances. Incomprehensible statements are said by nothing. She has already died. There is now only a vacuum where there was once a person."

The stage director Granville-Barker's verdict: "the mindless wraith that we see is no longer Ophelia" amounts to much the same thing. Well, most of us are not psychiatrists, and we do not know much about schizophrenia. That apart, is Laing's – or Granville-Barker's – verdict what we feel about Ophelia, here? It is always dangerous to make assumptions about madness in Shakespeare – particularly so in this play, where the hero himself adopts it as an alter ego to suit his purposes. In any event, one of Shakespeare's most beloved creations is the Fool (particularly in *King Lear*) who represents that eccentric commentary on the affairs of 'sane' men which casts light into the obscure corners of their doings and shows *them* often to be the real fools in life's drama. It is noticeable that in her 'madness' Ophelia's mind has a good deal of Hamlet's sharpness.

Horatio, generally a sound source, does not think that the mad Ophelia is "nothing". He is apprehensive that what she says "may strew/Dangerous conjectures in ill-breeding minds" (Act IV, scene 5, 14-15). Clearly there has been a good deal of pointed commentary in her ramblings about the state of affairs in Denmark, a suggestion anticipated in the résumé on her condition a few lines previously from a Gentleman, one of those characters whom Shakespeare inserts momentarily to direct our thoughts, and then is heard no more. "Her speech is nothing/Yet the unshapèd use of it doth move/The hearers to collection." (Act IV, scene 5, 7-9.)

The Gentleman tells us that "She speaks much of her father". But is that what she does throughout this scene? What are her first words on entering?

> Where is the beauteous majesty of Denmark?
> (Act IV, scene 5, 21)

It is an arresting, and at the same time beautiful line. It seems impossible that we are not meant to pause and ponder it. It seems to still the ferment of conjecture that has been stirred up by the Queen,

Gentleman and Horatio. Who is this beauteous majesty that has surfaced in Ophelia's mind? In spite of what the Gentleman has said, is there anything else in the rest of this scene that suggests that her father's death is at the root of her grief? (And in saying this, one must be objective about one's feeling that there *ought* not to be – since he has been directly and cruelly responsible for her present condition.) It is difficult to think that a father like Polonius, whom we have seen only in an authoritarian capacity in his relations with Ophelia, could somehow in her subconscious be metaphorically transfigured in this way.

Spencer suggests that Ophelia may merely mean: 'Where is the Queen?', or that she is addressing Gertrude directly: 'Where has your queenly beauty gone?'(i.e. in your present haggard, because conscience-stricken, state). But such a limited inquiry about Gertrude's state of cosmetic preservation does not carry a large enough meaning for the moment. And in the context of the age, whether we like it or not, "majesty" is more likely to signify a man. Gertrude is a queen consort, not a monarch. Ophelia may of course be referring to Denmark's rightful king – Hamlet – who is not so long afterwards to burst in on her interment announcing himself as "I, Hamlet the Dane."

There would be fittingness in this. Or it may be that Ophelia's line and the snatches of popular ballad with which she follows it, link in her wandering mind, the death of old Hamlet with her personal loss of his son as a lover.

> How should I your true-love know
> From another one?
>
> (Act IV, scene 5, 23-4)

The song is addressed directly to the Queen. Somewhere from the depths of her subconscious, Ophelia has dredged up a fragment of the terrible truth. The inescapable suggestion is the contrast between the 'true love' of Gertrude's first marriage and her 'other' one to the "mildewed ear" of Claudius. Gertrude appears at first not to take the inference. "Alas, sweet lady, what imports this song?" But the 'mad' Ophelia will not let her off the hook:

OPHELIA
Say you? Nay, pray you, mark.
(*Sings*)
   He is dead and gone, lady.
   He is dead and gone.
   At his head a grass-green turf,
   At his heels a stone.
O, ho!

Her 'true' love, her first husband, is in his grave, as surely as Ophelia's love, Hamlet, is totally dead to her. Gertrude's reaction, the panicky "Nay, but, Ophelia", suggests a recoil from an unpalatable truth that has been demonstrated to her.

Claudius enters at this point and this thread is lost. Interestingly, when he interprets Ophelia's first words to him, "Well, God dild [= reward] you! They say the owl was a baker's daughter" (a reference to a folk tale) as being "Conceit upon her father", she will have none of it: "Pray let's have no words of this …"

She now launches into a ballad of love and betrayal whose frank language has given the commentators some trouble, as being inconsistent with her innocent mind. A maid, believing herself to be the one true love of her Valentine's day suitor, allows herself to be sexually possessed by him – and is abandoned immediately afterwards. The lines are a neat encapsulation of the male take on such matters down the ages. 'Easy' girls may be nice to have around, but they are not promising marriage material.

   Alack, and fie for shame!
   Young men will do't, if they come to't.
   By Cock, they are to blame.

   Quoth she, 'Before you tumbled me,
     You promised me to wed.'
He answers:
   'So would I ha' done, by yonder sun,
     An thou hadst not come to my bed.'
                (Act IV, scene 5, 60-7)

This is not the language of a girl who is ignorant of the way the world wags. ("Cock", incidentally, here does double duty as slang for God and the penis). But there is nothing inconsistent in it as the observation (now free of inhibition in the dream state of her madness) of a young woman brought up in the company we have seen about her, in her family and the court. In a scene so often dismissed as being about a 'non' person, Shakespeare, in fact, makes Ophelia's 'wild' utterances extraordinarily pregnant with meaning. They alarm all those around her, and for widely differing reasons. Polonius is not, of course, present to savour the irony of a scenario in which his daughter seems to be imagining herself as having disobeyed him – and suffered the consequences. (Had he been, he would doubtless have managed, anyway, to misconstrue her song.) The deeper, tragic, irony for Ophelia is that in obeying him, she has also rejected Hamlet – with all the consequences that have followed.

It takes her death and funeral to shed light on the vexations and obscurities that have seemed to surround Hamlet's love for her, and her eligibility to enjoy it. In Hamlet's case the sight of her body in the grave provokes a violent upsurge of feeling and the restatement to Laertes of what we always knew to be true.

> I loved Ophelia. Forty thousand brothers
> Could not with all their quantity of love
> Make up my sum.
>
> (Act V, scene 1, 265-7)

There is absolute clarity at last. And since Gertrude has already said:

> I hoped thou shouldst have been my Hamlet's wife.
> I thought thy bride-bed to have decked, sweet maid,
> And not have strewed thy grave.
>
> (Act V, scene 1, 240-2)

it is quite clear that there was never any kind of hierarchical objection to the match along the lines of Polonius's assertions in Act II, scene 1. There was all along, it appears, 'no problem'. Ophelia's death seems to drive Hamlet almost mad with grief. He rages and storms against Laertes who has leapt into the grave.

> 'Swounds, show me what thou't do.
> Woo't weep? Woo't fight? Woo't fast? Woo't tear thyself?
> Woo't drink up eisel? Eat a crocodile?

I'll do't. Dost thou come here to whine?
To outface me with leaping in her grave?
Be buried quick with her, and so will I.
And if thou prate of mountains, let them throw
Millions of acres on us ...

(Act V, scene 1, 270-7)

This is one of the few moments in the play at which Hamlet seems genuinely unhinged and out of control. And he does not know all that we know. We, as it were, cannot share with him our sorrowful reflections on these appalling consequences of Polonius's wickedness and folly.

4

The Mind of Hamlet

As we have seen, Hamlet is the most loquacious character in Shakespeare. His philosophical nature dominates the play and makes it to an extraordinary degree *his* play. His entry to the action is keenly anticipated even before we see him. He is the key to unlocking the perturbing appearance of the Ghost in scene 1: "This spirit, dumb to us, will speak to him," says Horatio at Act I, scene 1, 172, and the watch breaks up in a keen anticipation of hearing his verdict on events as soon as Elsinore shall awake to the business of the day.

Yet, as we have also observed, many of Hamlet's mental concerns seem to have little to do with the tremendous events to whose centre the Ghost's revelations have propelled him. Right to the end in Act V when he has returned to Denmark, with the deaths of three of the play's characters on his head and in the full awareness that the King has signed his death warrant, he can spend 200 lines in delighted discourse on the meaning of life with two gravediggers, men of low degree whose opinions might not be thought likely to be of any interest at that juncture of the action. Yet Shakespeare does not think so, and he makes the encounter an ineradicably memorable one.

Hamlet's mind is here gloriously alive, and his democratic admiration of the gravedigger's wit is in marked contrast to, for example, his contempt for Polonius: "How absolute the knave is! We must speak by the card, or equivocation will undo us. By the Lord, Horatio, this three years I have took note of it, the age is grown so picked that the toe of the peasant comes so near the heel of the courtier he galls his kibe." (Act V, scene 1, 135-9) While Yorick, in the person of the remnant that is left of him – his skull – must be the only Shakespearean character who has vividly established his identity with the play-going public from the position of having been dead thirty years before the play in which he features begins.

> Alas, poor Yorick! I knew him,
> Horatio. A fellow of infinite jest, of most excellent fancy.
> He hath bore me on his back a thousand times. And now
> how abhorred in my imagination it is! My gorge rises at it.
> Here hung those lips that I have kissed I know not how oft.
> Where be your gibes now? Your gambols, your songs, your
> flashes of merriment that were wont to set the table on a
> roar? Not one now to mock your own grinning? Quite
> chop-fallen?
>
> (Act V, scene 1, 181-9)

Though set on the page as prose, these lines are pure poetry, and virtually impossible not to speak as such. And it is of a piece with the play of Hamlet's mind that the supreme pathos of this makes us laugh along with the dead spirit who will never do so again. In representation this can be made a grim scene, the skull of a beloved retainer being manhandled unceremoniously amid the spoil heaps of a grave that is being dug, in which, as we know, though Hamlet does not, Ophelia is shortly to be interred. But Shakespeare can take such a moment and transfigure it, so that we are transported for its duration outside and above the immediate exigencies and cares of the plot.

It is one of the great pities that, the economics of production being what they are (and human endurance being what it is), a great deal of this metaphysical ratiocination and homespun wisdom must be cut out in the theatre, in the interest of 'getting on' with the drama. Not only the most discussed of Shakespeare's plays, *Hamlet* is, at more than four hours, easily his longest. Very few productions of it are not based on a substantially cut text. And where cuts are made they inevitably fall on the philosophical digressions that are seen to hold up – as indeed they do – the action. A man standing for such long periods stock still, while he shares with us the contents of his mind on issues of life, death and the nature of the universe, is not the easiest of propositions for a stage director. Even Hamlet's most famous soliloquies are liable to find themselves subject to trimming, if not downright omission.

The result of this has tended to concentrate our view of Hamlet solely on his character in terms of the action to which the play apparently compels him, and to make us lose sight of the remarkable mind that operates independently of the plot. Under these pressures it is not surprising that in production Hamlet the Renaissance man, and wit, has so often given way to Hamlet the Romantic hero/victim of circumstances, an easier proposition to represent in performance. And Hamlet's famous melancholy, in which, as the Arden Shakespeare editor Harold Jenkins points out, he gives vent to many of the ideas which were simply part of the common intellectual currency of the age (Timothy Bright's *Treatise of Melancholy*, 1586, might well have been among influences) becomes a personal quality, to be interpreted in the context of the neuroses which contemporary society recognises in itself.

Hamlet the wit

Our first glimpse of Hamlet catches him indeed in a mood of cryptic truculence rather than of Romantic self-pity. His opening remark to Claudius, who has belatedly addressed him (having pointedly devoted himself first to the affairs of Laertes): "But now, my cousin Hamlet, and my son – " (Act I scene 2, 64) is of a piece with that love of fine distinctions, philosophical, linguistic and moral, that characterises him throughout. The Penguin editor makes Hamlet's riposte "A little more than kin, and less than kind!" an aside. Not all editions do. In any event, its substance is more important than the question of whether or not Claudius is meant to hear it.

Hamlet has decided to take issue with both the letter and spirit of Claudius's attempt to ingratiate himself with him. The fine detail of Hamlet's dissent is likely to escape us in performance – as it almost certainly does Claudius to whom it is addressed. Yet it is worth trying to follow the terms in which it is couched. First, in calling his stepson "cousin" Claudius affronts Hamlet who claims a much closer relationship than that of a mere kinsman, which the term implies. And when Claudius belatedly tacks on to this his acknowledgement of the relationship of "son", Hamlet chooses to be affronted on that score, too. The "kind" on which he insists implies not only the profound sense of community that stems from being of immediate family, but of being of kindred disposition and nature (a term profoundly important in Shakespeare and never more so than in *Hamlet* and *King Lear*). Hamlet's quibble makes it clear that he distances himself from any such feelings for Claudius.

These are Hamlet's first words, and Shakespeare is not given to betraying his audiences when it comes to first impressions, whether they are delivered by the protagonist or by a third party commentator. Here he has Hamlet establishing a distinctive approach to the human universe about him that is to set the tone for his subsequent dealings with it. And it is characteristic of Shakespeare/Hamlet this is accomplished through a highly concentrated argument whose subtleties will be wholly lost on Claudius.

The quibble intensifies in Hamlet's riposte to his uncle's inquiry after his mental state:

> KING
>> How is it that the clouds still hang on you?
> HAMLET
>> Not so, my lord. I am too much in the sun.
>> (Act I, scene 2, 66-7)

This is not merely, as it appears to be, an objection from Hamlet that he feels himself to be forbidden his right of grieving, and forced into too close a proximity to the gaiety of the court and the sunshine of the king's blessing – though undoubtedly his words will quite satisfactorily sustain that interpretation. To acquire the double layer of irony in Hamlet's meaning we must refer to a similar usage in *King Lear* (Act II, scene 2). Kent, in the guise of a servant of Lear, has been placed in the stocks by the Duke of Cornwall. Ruminating on the changes in his fortune, from Earl to King's retainer, and now to lowly minion, to be humiliated out of hand, he refers to a proverb familiar to the time, but now passed out of the language:

> KENT
>> Good king, that must approve the common saw,
>> Thou out of Heaven's benediction comest
>> To the warm sun.

There is a clear echo here of the notion stated as early as John Heywood's *Proverbs* of 1546: "In your running from him to me, yee run/Out of God's blessing into the warme sun", a usage that is in frequent use thereafter. It is not surprising that a sun-worshipping age such as ours will not immediately infer from these lines, which sound a little paradoxical in our ears, their meaning which was so clear to Shakespeare's audience, and intended by Hamlet – that he has, in fact, in the wake of his father's death, come from a universally respected state to one that is inferior and despised.

Obtusely oblivious to any of this, Claudius continues prosing. Hamlet's grief for his dead father is "unmanly", "a fault to heaven,/ A fault against the dead, a fault to nature" (Act I, scene 2, 101-2). Hamlet ignores him. His curt reply, "I shall in all my best obey you, madam" (Act I, scene 2, 120) is solely for his mother's benefit.

Not, of course, that she escapes his censure. To Hamlet her marriage has become inextricably associated with that something "rotten in the state of Denmark" of which the Ghost's appearance is shortly to furnish evidence, if not to Hamlet's mind at that juncture, absolute proof.

The impact of the Ghost

As we saw earlier, Hamlet's truculent passivity is dispelled by Horatio's relation to him of the Ghost's intervention in the affairs of Elsinore. Yet even in the fever of anticipation in which he joins Horatio and Marcellus in their watch on the battlements, as King Claudius carouses below to an accompanying cannonade, the philosopher runs ahead of the man of action. As they await the entry of the apparition, in, as we may imagine, a state of the utmost tension, Hamlet finds time – and, more remarkably, the mental space – to ruminate aloud on the nature of the moral evil that has not merely given rise to Claudius's corrupt stewardship of the Danish state, but also represents a universal threat to human integrity. A "vicious mole of nature" (Act I, scene 4, 24), beginning in the propensity to drunkenness, has, like some deadly bacillus, spread throughout the King's entire personality, "breaking down the pales and forts of reason". The result is to expose the individual, and in this case the state that is inextricably a part of his moral being, to "general censure". Thomas Nashe, *Pierce Penniless*, (1592) and Robert Greene, *Pandosto*, (1588) are among the sources for this characteristically Renaissance viewpoint. A contemporary audience might well have inferred a reference to the recent downfall of Elizabeth's popular favourite the Earl of Essex. Not a few commentators have said that Shakespeare intended us to take it as applicable to Hamlet himself.

I said above that Hamlet was ruminating aloud. For one seriously wonders whether Horatio and Marcellus, both on the alert for the Ghost, are actually listening to his lecture expliqué. The text is corrupt here, with a plethora of meanings presenting themselves. The Penguin edition adopts a reading that suggests Hamlet's being interrupted by Horatio as he progresses to the next level of his argument.

> The dram of evil
> Doth all the noble substance of a doubt,
> To his own scandal –
> *Enter the Ghost*

HORATIO
> Look, my lord, it comes.
> (Act I scene 4, 36-8)

It is a moment of the utmost tension. We must consider that to an Elizabethan sensibility the appearance of a spirit such as Shakespeare's creation here would mean far more than it does to us, long inured to ghosts from the 18th-century gothic novel, generations of Victorian and Edwardian short-story collections and decades of scary movies and TV dramas.

For the English mind as it was at the turn of the 16th century ghosts offered several possibilities. A Roman Catholic would accept that they might be spirits of the dead, permitted for some significant purpose, probably one of communication with the living, to return from Purgatory. To a Protestant, unable to avail himself of a Purgatory no longer part of the reformed doctrine, such spirits had, inevitably, to come directly from Heaven or Hell. And as King James I's influential treatise *Daemonologie* of 1597 makes quite clear, the balance of probability was almost always regarded as tilting towards the latter. A third position, argued in Reginald Scot's *Discoverie of Witchcraft* (1584) and its accompanying *Discourse upon Divels and Spirits*, was complete scepticism. Scot was not an agnostic: for him the spirit exists, but it cannot assume material form. Evidence that it does can only be an imposition by trickery on enfeebled or overwrought minds. (Hamlet's mental state might be thought to fall into the latter category, but there is not the faintest suggestion of it here.) Scot's views, which of course bordered boldly on heresy, had few followers either in his own age or for many years thereafter, and his book was proscribed by King James.

Another important point is that in Shakespearean drama the Ghost has been elevated to become far more than the stock puppet figure of so much earlier Elizabethan theatre, a borrowing from Seneca, popping up like some Jack-in-the-Box, to be greeted by the audience at best with oohs and ahs, at worst with derision. In *Hamlet* Shakespeare has made his Ghost an instrument of terror. Although Hamlet had, as he thought, prepared himself for this encounter in Act I, scene 2, he is palpably appalled by the apparition. His instinctive reaction is not a welcome, but a prayer for deliverance from evil. "Angels and ministers of grace defend us!" (Act I, scene 4, 39). And this is reinforced by the conviction that this appearance can only mean that something unfathomably bad is on foot.

> What may this mean
> That thou, dead corse, again in complete steel,
> Revisits thus the glimpses of the moon,
> Making night hideous, and we fools of nature
> So horridly to shake our disposition
> With thoughts beyond the reaches of our souls?
>
> (Act I, scene 4, 51-6)

In earlier plays, *Richard III* and *Julius Caesar*, ghostly apparitions had been very largely embedded in the subconscious of those to whom they appeared. For King Richard and Brutus they are somewhat in the category of nightmares, and in both cases echo bad conscience. In the later *Macbeth*, the ghost of Banquo is palpably an extension of Macbeth's own mind, come to rebuke him for a specific evil deed. But in *Hamlet*, the Ghost cannot be attributed to the protagonist's state of mind or a bad conscience. For one thing he has been seen – first seen indeed – by others. Psychologically speaking, there is nothing 'local' about him, as far as Hamlet is concerned. He comes in as the harbinger of a general evil, the struggle against which is to drive the entire course of the drama.

Indeed, at the outset Hamlet addresses the Ghost not as his father, but rather as a spirit that represents his father. Even after the Ghost has asserted his identity to him, "I am thy father's spirit" (Act I, scene 5, 9), he remains for Hamlet "poor ghost" (Act I, scene 5, 96) and "an honest ghost" (Act I, scene 5, 138). Doubts about his origin continue to recur for Hamlet: He is still vacillating at Act II, scene 2, 596-7, "The spirit that I have seen/May be a devil", and it is not until the King's reaction to the Gonzago play that we see him finally convinced. "O good Horatio, I'll take the ghost's word for a /thousand pound." (Act III, scene 2, 295-6.)

Yet the effect of the Ghost's appearance in Act I is to steel Hamlet's nerve to action. A cloudy, peripheral figure in the council chamber scene, he sloughs off rumination and comes boldly to centre stage. It is now Horatio and Marcellus who are the doubters. "What if it tempt you toward the flood, my lord" (Act I, scene 4, 69), his old friend anxiously exclaims when the Ghost indicates that his desire is an audience à deux with Hamlet. He shrugs off their attempts to restrain him. "Unhand me, gentlemen./By heaven, I'll make a ghost of him that lets [= hinders] me!" (Act I, scene 4, 84-5). This is the first we see of Hamlet the man of action. Yet the man of action is the constant companion to the philosophy student who, apparently, cannot make up his mind to act. Time after time in the play, we see him, without giving the matter a second thought, dispose of those who are a threat to him – Polonius, Rosencrantz, Guildenstern – until, in the final scene the Augean stables of evil that are Claudius's creation in Elsinore are cleansed in one swift, terrible reckoning.

For the moment, Hamlet confronts his father's apparition in a state of clear-eyed fearlessness. Interestingly, to the student Hamlet lately come back from that seat of the Reformation, Wittenberg, his father chooses not one of the Protestant options available to him as the explanation of his embodiment – Heaven or Hell – but something that is recognisably the Catholic Purgatory.

> I am thy father's spirit,
> Doomed for a certain term to walk the night,
> And for the day confined to fast in fires,
> Till the foul crimes done in my days of nature
> Are burnt and purged away.
>
> (Act I, scene 5, 9-13)

As we have seen, Hamlet withstands the Ghost's recital without turning a hair.

As a body, receiving a wound, goes into shock as a delayed

reaction, so his mind at first copes with these revelations without sustaining damage. It is only with the departure of the apparition of his father that he is brought down to earth, to the world in which such things must be explained to (or kept from) these friends who have, anyway, no power to help him. He is suddenly and utterly alone, in a universe of revelation set apart from Horatio and Marcellus.

The "wild and whirling words" (Horatio, Act I, scene 5, 133) with which Hamlet addresses his friends in the aftermath of the Ghost's departure are, of course, a necessary device, while he wonders how much he dare impart to anyone of what he has just learnt from the Ghost. He is about, so it seems, to tell Horatio what he has seen and heard, but the presence of Marcellus inhibits him, restricting him to the apparently banal inconsequentiality of: "There's never a villain dwelling in all Denmark –/But he's an arrant knave." (Act I, scene 5, 123-4). Yet the harum-scarum business of the rest of this scene, with the Ghost, mysteriously everywhere beneath the stage, backing up his injunctions to secrecy, is also a mirror to the fevered state of Hamlet's mind, as the revelation of his uncle's wickedness and his mother's perfidy sinks in, threatening for a moment to overwhelm his mind.

It is important at this moment that we fully understand that his famous injunction

> There are more things in heaven and earth, Horatio,
> Than are dreamt of in your philosophy.
>
> (Act I, scene 5, 166-7)

(which, like "To thine own self be true ..." is often quoted out of context and misunderstood) is not for one moment to be taken as a patronising one. It is not a lofty assumption of superiority over his old friend. "Philosophy", here, means natural philosophy, i.e. science (as indeed it was styled in some chairs of science in British universities well into the last century). The use of "your" is not personal, implying some inferior level of understanding in Horatio, but colloquial – as it later is in the assessment of that sound tradesman the Gravedigger: "your water is a sore decayer of your whoreson dead body." (Act V, scene 1, 168-9). Hamlet means merely that what has happened tonight goes beyond the power of science to explain it. As Hamlet contemplates the abyss of evil to whose edge the Ghost has drawn him, his mood is the very reverse of patronising. He knows that he has entered a world where, for him as surely as for Horatio, science can furnish no answers.

The antic disposition

In the face of this sea of uncertainty the assumption of the "antic disposition" is, far from being a symptom of mental infirmity, an act of ingenious self-determination by Hamlet. It creates something of a holding position, enabling him to inhabit a parallel mental universe from which to observe the denizens of Denmark's court, while he ponders all the implications of his father's appearance to him. Certainly it would be difficult to sustain for a mind not fully under its own control. When adopting it Hamlet's mind is, as Kitto points out, conspicuously clear and quick. We feel a play of intellect belonging to carefree past days of student wrangling and contests of wit – whose subject matter might range from the metaphysical to the sexual. It loves moral digressions, and we can even agree with Schlegel that Hamlet " ... has a natural inclination for crooked ways". He runs rings round Polonius. Act II, scene 2, 173ff is characteristic. Piquing himself on his sagacity, Polonius has been assuring the King and Gertrude that he will "board" Hamlet (i.e. lay alongside him as a pirate craft does its prize) and plunder the truth from him.

> POLONIUS
> Do you know me, my lord?
> HAMLET
> Excellent well. You are a fishmonger.
> POLONIUS
> Not I, my lord.
> HAMLET
> Then I would you were so honest a man.

In being taken incongruously for a man whose trade advertises his following so pungently to the nostrils, Polonius is made to look ridiculous. His courtier's robes are turned by the notion in an instant to the stallholder's odoriferous apron, covered in fish scales, fish guts and blood. Hamlet's sneer, reinforced by his later allusion to "maggots in a dead dog", also suggests to us the stench of corruption that emanates from Polonius. And even the complacent courtier cannot be unaware that "fishmonger" doubles here as "fleshmonger" i.e., pimp. And this seems to us appropriate enough as applied to one who, as we know, is shortly to "loose" his daughter to Hamlet like a female farm animal in heat to a male in rut, while he eavesdrops on the outcome from behind an arras. From a number of contemporary sources we know also that fishmongers were also popularly thought to have particularly seductive and fertile wives and daughters, whose wantonness made them especially prone to breed with all and sundry. Such a humiliating notion seems peculiarly appropriate to one so furtively, yet impotently, curious as Polonius is about the sex lives of his children.

I do not know whether or not it is a coincidence, but the antic disposition seems to function with peculiar felicity in the vicinity of the person of Polonius. He is the butt of Hamlet's first trial of it, above. His death prompts the last exercise of its powers in Act IV. After that we hear no more of it. But Shakespeare ensures that the antic disposition takes its leave of us on a high note. The subject is Polonius, but it is the King's turn to be the target:

KING
 Now, Hamlet, where's Polonius?
HAMLET
 At supper.
KING
 At supper? Where?
HAMLET
 Not where he eats, but where 'a is eaten. A certain
 convocation of politic worms are e'en at him. Your worm is
 your only emperor for diet. We fat all creatures else to fat
 us, and we fat ourselves for maggots. Your fat king and
 your lean beggar is but variable service –
                         (Act IV, scene 3, 16-24)

The King, his lackeys Rosencrantz and Guildenstern, and even Gertrude have but one practical concern in such a serious situation as the mysterious death of such a senior minister: where is the body of Polonius? Hamlet, here the Wittenberg student par excellence, plays with them all, parrying the king's inquiry with a display of wit and historical erudition that the desperately anxious monarch is doubtless in no mood to appreciate. In a passage of allusiveness concentrated even by Shakespearean standards, the worms that are at work consuming the body of Polonius have become also councillors at Worms on the Rhine, seat of the diet (Diät – the assembly) of the Holy Roman Empire where, in 1521 Luther was summoned to affirm or deny his Protestant doctrines before Charles V. The wonderful juxtaposition of the earth-shaking historical confrontation on the one hand, and the steady munching of maggots on a corpse, is one of antic Hamlet's finest distillations.

The poetry of Hamlet

To a very great extent (the Act I, Scene 1 speech of Marcellus being one notable exception) the memorable poetry of *Hamlet* is the poetry of Hamlet himself. The power of his mind, acting either under the pressure of events, or simply in reaction to the mystery of existence as he contemplates it, informs much of the play. His major verse soliloquies punctuate its action right up to the later stages of Act IV. But they are backed up by numerous other philosophical reflections to others in both prose (which is generally of itself of a highly poetical nature) and verse, on topics ranging from the troubled human universe to Rosencrantz and Guildenstern, to his tips on acting and direction to the Players. As we have seen, few stage productions in our time can encompass all of these things in their entirety.

Like his creator, Hamlet is able to clothe his thoughts with vivid images. (It is tempting to say that he must, at times, more resemble Shakespeare than any other of Shakespeare's characters.) Thus, the sheer concentration of "O, most wicked speed, To post/With such dexterity to incestuous sheets!" (Act I, scene 2, 156-7) expresses with peculiar sting the nature of his mother's sexual betrayal of his father (down to the physical unpleasantness of it all as perceived by Hamlet – his mother's body now unnaturally polluting Denmark's royal bed linen with the semen of her first husband's brother).

This, the first of Hamlet's soliloquies, is germane to the action. It acts as a powerful antidote to the impression of Claudius's marriage which that usurping monarch has sedulously sought to inculcate in his court in the first part of the scene. But Hamlet is quite capable of stilling the action altogether, while he ruminates on some aspect of existence that is preoccupying him, quite outside the immediate circumstances of the play. The most celebrated of his soliloquies,

"To be, or not to be" (Act III, scene 1, 56ff), acts almost as a brake on what is happening at that point, as we, with the King and Polonius, wait to see what will be the outcome of the encounter between Hamlet and the approaching Ophelia. One can almost share a director's despair as he or she bows to the necessity of including this most famous rumination at such a dramatic juncture.

The speech appears to have no direct connection with what might be going on in Hamlet's mind vis à vis the action of the play at this point. True, an echo of the Act I, scene 2 soliloquy, "O that this too too sullied flesh would melt", with its lines "Or that the Everlasting had not fixed/His canon 'gainst self slaughter", may perhaps be inferred from Hamlet's opening proposition here. Certainly, the list of commentators who have assumed that "To be or not to be" refers to suicide is a long and distinguished one, and includes both Bradley and Dover Wilson. But is that assumption sustainable from the text? Whereas Act I, scene 2 is an intensely personal utterance, in which Hamlet's anguished reflections on his mother's behaviour continually surface to torment him, "To be, or not to be" is conducted almost throughout in an atmosphere of dispassionate philosophical enquiry.

The substance of the soliloquy is rooted in ideas with which any reasonably well-read individual (not necessarily a scholar) of Shakespeare's era would have been familiar. Discussions on death and the fear of death; death-as-sleep; the frightening possibility of dreams in the death state; the impossibility of returning from the death state, in sources ranging from Socrates and Plutarch to Montaigne, who regarded death as "an amendment and entrance into a long and quiet night", were readily available in English translation (here, John Florio's). The publication in 1573 by the Earl of Oxford of Thomas Bedingfield's translation of the 16th-century Italian doctor and mathematician Girolamo Cardano's *De Consolatione*, as *Cardanus' Comforts* provided enquiring readers with a text which became fundamental to the age. For Cardano, as for Montaigne, death will be a sleep in which "we dream nothing".

This kinship between death and sleep which so fascinated the Renaissance surfaces time and time again in Shakespeare's plays. We find it occurring in contexts ranging from the disgusted reaction to Sly's drunken slumber in The *Taming of Shrew*: "O monstrous beast! How like a swine he lies./Grim death how foul and loathsome is thine image" (Induction, scene 1); through the Duke's cynical survey to the condemned Claudio of the fate awaiting Man in *Measure for Measure*: "Thy best of rest is sleep,/And that thou oft provok'st [provok'st = wish for]; yet grossly fear'st/Thy death which is no more" (Act III, scene 1); to Macduff's urgent clarion call to Macbeth's guests on the discovery of Duncan's murder: "Awake!/Shake off this downy sleep, death's counterfeit,/And look on death itself!" (Act II, scene 3).

Hamlet, however, illuminates this meditation on a familiar theme with the full force of his dramatic imagination:

> To die, to sleep –
> To sleep – perchance to dream. Ay, there's the rub.
> For in that sleep of death what dreams may come
> When we have shuffled off this mortal coil
> Must give us pause.
>
> (Act III, scene 1, 64-8)

There is for him no consolation in the quiet assurances of Montaigne or Cardano. Montaigne's "quiet night" may well turn out to be a condition of unmitigated terror, and Man, on this side of the portals that give entrance to it, is constantly in "dread of something after death" (Act III, scene 1, 78).

But, to return to Hamlet's opening proposition which has given rise to this meditation:

> To be, or not to be – that is the question;
> Whether 'tis nobler in the mind to suffer
> The slings and arrows of outrageous fortune
> Or to take arms against a sea of troubles
> And by opposing end them.
>
> (Act III, scene 1, 56-60)

In this much-discussed play, these are certainly the most discussed lines. As I have said, the list of critics who have assumed that the topic here is whether or not Hamlet should commit suicide is long and illustrious. And our Penguin editor concurs, though toying with an alternative explanation: "Is there an after life or not?" Somewhat oddly he prefers not to adopt his proposed alternative on the grounds that: "This, though congruous with the line of thought later in the soliloquy, is more difficult to communicate on the stage." It seems strange to suggest that an actor or director might balk at trying to convey Shakespeare's line of thought, let alone change its meaning, on the grounds that an audience might not understand what is intended. It seems to me that reference back to "O that this too too sullied flesh should melt" does not help us here. That was a personal expostulation forced from Hamlet in reaction to circumstances. The "question" proposed here is surely nothing specifically to do with Hamlet (or a Hamlet suicide), but the wider one of whether or not human existence has any value. Whether we might all, in fact, be better off dead? And as a corollary – is death in any event so frightful? That much, I feel sure, is inescapable. The difficulties really begin with the second part of this opening: "Whether 'tis nobler in the mind ..." Either we may patiently submit to whatever nastinesses life throws at us, or – what? Taking arms "against a sea of troubles" cannot be made to mean suicide, however we look at it, in spite of the apparent finality of "end them". And surely a mind like Shakespeare's cannot be suggesting that if we 'stand up' for ourselves in the face of our troubles we will vanquish them all in the end. This would be to turn Shakespeare into Kipling and reduce the argument to the level of that poet's *If*, with its wholesome conclusion "You'll be a Man my son". Clearly, Victorian notions of what constitutes being a "Man" are no part of Hamlet's complex sensibility. "Man", for Hamlet, means mankind.

Does Hamlet therefore mean the opposite: namely that if we "take arms" against this "sea of troubles" (battling with weapons against the watery element is, admittedly, not the most easily assimilable of images) we will, in the end, be overwhelmed, but our death will not be an ignoble one? Will it release us from "The heartache and the thousand natural shocks/That flesh is heir to."? Perhaps. But no sooner has Hamlet arrived at this apparent "consummation/Devoutly to be wished" than the potential horrors of this, too, come bursting in on him, envisaged with all the poetic power of his hyperactive mind.

It is part of Hamlet/Shakespeare's genius that to wring the maximum impact from this juxtaposition, the awfulness of life is first depicted in graphic terms. Who would not want, he asks us, to escape, for whatever destination, life's concatenation of evils: "the whips and scorns of time,/Th'oppressor's wrong, the proud man's contumely,/The pangs of despised love, the law's delay,/The insolence of office, and the spurns/That patient merit of th'unworthy takes"?

In Act III, scene 1 of *Measure for Measure* Claudio, condemned to death by a new and harsh regime in his native Vienna for getting "his friend with child", i.e. making pregnant his lover, has an immediate answer.

> Ay but to die and go we know not where
> To lie in cold obstruction and to rot
> This sensible warm motion to become
> A kneaded clod and the delighted spirit
> To bathe in fiery floods, or to reside
> In thrilling region of thick ribbèd ice.

Claudio, a young man not given to profound thought, is nevertheless stirred to a form of rude eloquence where his own fate is concerned. His answer is highly effective in its concrete imagery. This afterlife is a Hell, as depicted in a painting of Bosch or Breughel. It will undoubtedly be a place of extreme discomfort, of the buckets-of-boiling-oil school of torment, and the soul condemned to it will be in for a bad time. These are images to which the sensibility of the northern European Renaissance would have been familiar from its gothic church doorways, with their troops of sinners being haled down to hell by armies of demons. Hamlet's answer to his own question is of a very different kidney. The terror of the afterlife lies in its very inscrutability. What we do not know frightens us far more than the caricature horrors represented by the fantasies of Claudio. For Hamlet these certainties are replaced by:

> the dread of something after death,
> The undiscovered country, from whose bourn
> No traveller returns

And it is this that

> puzzles the will,
> And makes us rather bear those ills we have
> Than fly to others that we know not of?
> (Act III, scene 1, 78-82)

There is to be no consolation here in any such notion as that death is merely a sleep. Man is to be constantly tormented by his apprehension of it. In "Thus conscience does makes cowards of us all", "conscience" means, not the faculty of moral insight that enables us to see right from wrong and acts as a brake on our living by the latter. Hamlet is here talking not of the consequences of sin on our chances in the afterlife, but rather of the fearful burden that Man as an imaginatively conscious being constantly bears with him in his earthly existence.

The generosity of Hamlet

Given the unsparing nature of Hamlet's wit throughout the play it is perhaps not surprising that little has been made of the co-existing, over-arching generosity of his mind. Yet he might be describing himself when he says of mankind:

> What a piece of work is a man, how noble in reason, how
> infinite in faculties, in form and moving how express and
> admirable, in action how like an angel, in apprehension
> how like a god: the beauty of the world, the paragon of
> animals!
>
> (Act II, scene 2, 303-7)

Even in the perception that accompanies that, namely that "this goodly frame the earth" has become a "sterile promontory", it is instinctive in him to seek to see the best in people. Here he greets Rosencrantz and Guildenstern, sent by the King to spy on him, in terms of the affectionate good fellowship of student days. To him, before they shall prove themselves otherwise, they are the "excellent good friends" and "good lads" (Act II, scene 2, 224, 226) he has always known. And a passage of humorously indecent undergraduate banter follows, as he revels in leading them to the suggestion that their situation in life – neither on the "very button" of "Fortune's cap", nor "the soles of her shoe" – is "about her waist, or in the middle of her favours?" They are happy to catch his tone – "Faith, her privates we" (i.e. mere private soldiers, the lowest form of military life; or intimate counsellors; or 'private parts – sexual organs).

To Laertes in Act V (an equally undeserving cause since Ophelia's brother is already in cahoots with Claudius to murder him), he extends the same immediate generosity. To Horatio, as the pair of them crouch in the graveyard and look in wonder as Ophelia's funeral cortege approaches, he elevates Laertes, without any evidence, as "a very noble youth" (Act V, scene 1, 220). After the graveside scuffle he confesses with generous perception: "I am very sorry, good Horatio,/ That to Laertes I forgot myself./For by the image of my cause I see/ The portraiture of his" (Act V, scene 2, 75-8). Finally, before the fencing match itself he makes to Laertes himself the totally unconditional apology. "Give me your pardon, sir./I have done you wrong." (Act V, scene 2, 220.)

It is of a piece with his careless generosity in refusing to "peruse the foils" before the fatal denouement. As Laertes anxiously shuffles the weapons on offer to the pair of them, to make sure that, as previously plotted with the king, he has the "unbated" rapier, (i.e. one without a button or some other blunting device on its point – which Laertes has furthermore anointed with poison to make sure nothing is left to chance), Hamlet is magnificently unaware of the intended treachery. It is simply not in his nature to go back on the apology he has just made to Laertes and question his good faith.

5

Denmark: politics and geopolitics

Two questions confront us when we think of the political entity that is the Denmark of *Hamlet*. The first is: what kind of state is Denmark, that is to say what are the rules for the transfer of power? Is it a hereditary monarchy of the type Shakespearean audiences would, of course, have instinctively understood – indeed it would have been the *only* system they understood. In which case Hamlet has clearly been defrauded of a throne. Or is it an elective system, such as is apparently clearly implied (or is it?) in Hamlet's angry remark at Act V, scene 2, 64-5: "He that hath .../Popped in between th'election and my hopes."?

Secondly: what kind of geopolitical system is Denmark operating in? Is it simply a unitary sovereign state? Or is it part of some kind of maritime empire or confederation, along the lines of the North Sea empire of the Danish King Cnut, who in 1016 was elected King of England where he is better known in history and mythology as King Canute? (He was also King of Norway for a period.) There do, in the play, seem to be interconnecting relations between the three states. When Claudius wants to get Hamlet out of the way, seeing him as a political threat following his killing of Polonius, he has recourse to England as a solution to his problems, rather as a vassal province than as a foreign sovereign state. We are not apparently to be in the slightest bit surprised that the authorities in England (whoever they are) will carry out an instruction to murder the heir to the Danish throne without batting an eyelid. The Norwegian monarchy appears to be closely related in blood to that of Denmark. And when, at the end of the play, a Norwegian prince, Fortinbras, comes on stage for the first time and calmly picks up the reins of the Danish state, no one seems to think that there is anything untoward in it.

The geopolitical concerns of a Denmark which is by virtue of its geographical situation both a North Sea and a Baltic state are borne in on us at the outset of the play in the discussion between Marcellus and Horatio about the nature of the Ghost. In a past which is fresh in the memory of Hamlet's young friend, old Hamlet has been involved in wars both against Norway and Poland:

> HORATIO
> Such was the very armour he had on
> When he the ambitious Norway combated.
> So frowned he once, when, in an angry parle,
> He smote the sledded Polacks on the ice.
> (Act I, scene 1, 60-3)

I say Poland. In the Penguin edition Spencer, unlike most editors, opts for the reading of "poleaxe", rather than "Polacks" at line 63, a reading he defends skilfully enough in a long note. The texts are dubious. Q2 and F1 read respectively "pollax" and "Pollax" – which could mean anything. Quite apart from anything else, elsewhere in the play the Poles (later, again the target of military operations) are referred to again as "Polacks" (a term long used in the United States – that great importer of 17th-century English usages). In this instance it seems to me that we have to take the kind of leap of imagination that was supplied by Alexander Pope in his edition of Shakespeare which appeared in 1725. Pope's edition certainly has its shortcomings, but in supplying the reading "Polacks" here, it does seem to come at what Shakespeare intended. The Penguin/Spencer version – "in an angry parle/He smote the sledded poleaxe on the ice" – simply gives us an angry old man bashing his weapon against the ground during a heated negotiation. The notion of smiting is surely that of raining blows on an enemy, not merely rapping the frozen ground in a fit of pique. The satisfying rout of sleigh-borne Polish troops in some frozen Baltic skirmish sits far more convincingly with the martial character and exploits of old Hamlet than that we are given by Spencer.

Horatio is to return to this conflict with Norway almost immediately after the first entry of the Ghost. In a display of his knowledge of current affairs to the simple soldiers Marcellus and Barnardo he gives us chapter and verse (Act I, scene 1, 79-107) on the political situation as it bears on the feverish preparation for military action which we can sense all round us. At some point in the past the balance of power between Norway and Denmark was decided by single combat between Hamlet senior and the Norwegian king, Old Fortinbras, in which the latter was killed and some territorial concessions were made. It is, as Spencer points out in his commentary to the Penguin edition, a solution that harks back to some heroic age in which kings were their countries' champions. It is in marked contrast to the atmosphere of cautious diplomacy that characterises the court of Claudius.

It is to that court that we must go in the following scene to have those details left out by Horatio filled in for us. Interestingly, as in Denmark, the throne of Norway did not pass on the king's death to Fortinbras's son, young Fortinbras, but to his brother "old Norway". In marked contrast to the philosopher Hamlet, the dead Norwegian king's son is hell-bent on action, in this case reversing the decision of single combat by resort to force of arms, behind his uncle's back.

To give Claudius his due, he here acquits himself as a sound diplomat. Faced with the importunate demands of young Fortinbras for "the surrender of those lands/ Lost by his father" (Act I, scene 2, 23-4), and knowing full well that the hot-headed young prince is acting without the king of Norway's say-so or even knowledge, he dispatches his envoys Cornelius and Voltemand on a civil, but at the same time clever, mission, to point out to the bedridden Norwegian king what is going on, and to ask him to forestall it.

Is all this – which occupies a good deal of stage time – of vast importance to the action as it concerns the issue between Claudius and Hamlet? Does it even greatly interest Shakespeare? Perhaps not. It is, of course, something he inherits from *Hamlet*'s predecessor plays and, like Prospero's lengthy explanation to Miranda in *The Tempest*, is something that has to be got through in speeches of greater length than a stage performance can generally bear. Its only function is to bring in Fortinbras at the end without our wondering where on earth he has sprung from. But Shakespeare is craftsman enough not to leave loose ends. In spite of the press of business afflicting Claudius's stewardship of the state, he is able to bring back Voltemand and Cornelius in Act II, scene 2, with their report of 'mission accomplished'. Except for the fact that they later provide further philosophical reflections for Hamlet – in this case on the futility of the life of the 'Man of Action' – the affairs of Denmark, Norway, Poland as countries with a stake in the geopolitics of the Baltic littoral are of no further concern to him or us.

Kenneth Branagh's film – discussed in Alan Sinfield's Penguin introduction — in which the theme of the play becomes the long-meditated conquest of Denmark by Fortinbras while the kingdom is beset by internal quarrels, is a perfectly legitimate director's 'take' on the events of *Hamlet*. But it diminishes the philosophical grandeur of the play to the level of a discussion about state security. Bacon, had he been a playwright, might have written a drama on such a theme, but not the author of *Hamlet*.

From the return of the ambassadors from Norway the political concerns of the play, such as they are, are internal. In securing his succession to the dead Hamlet, Claudius has engineered, as he sees it, a state of political stability. From his point of view, knowing nothing of Hamlet junior's sources of insight into his means of attaining it, the sole question is: will Hamlet accept that? The court and council, as we saw in Chapter 2, appear to. But throughout the play Claudius seems to have recurring doubts. Even after the killing of Polonius he is wary of moving against Hamlet because of his perceived popular appeal: "He's loved of the distracted multitude." (Act IV, scene 3, 4) Claudius may be a bad man, but he is no fool. He knows how to keep political opponents off-balance as we saw in his neutralising the threat of young Fortinbras. It is a cunning move to send for two old friends of Hamlet in his quest to get to the bottom of his nephew's sudden strange behaviour. Does he already know that Rosencrantz and Guildenstern are readily corruptible? As with Laertes (and, before the play opens, Gertrude), he seems to have an instinct for such things. The terms of their reply to his request to them "to gather/So much as from occasion you may glean,/Whether aught to us unknown afflicts him thus" (Act II, scene 2, 15-17) are so unctuous that we have our doubts about any trust Hamlet might repose in them.

> ROSENCRANTZ
> Both your majesties
> Might, by the sovereign power you have of us,
> Put your dread pleasures more into command

Than to entreaty.
GUILDENSTERN
      But we both obey,
And here give up ourselves in the full bent
To lay our service freely at your feet,
To be commanded.

                         (Act II, scene 2, 26-32)

This goes far beyond what might be a necessary, but still dignified, expression of compliance to a king's request from young men in a certain state of life (who also happen to be his nephew's friends). Certainly, after his first impulsively generous reception of them, Hamlet realises very swiftly that these companions of his youth have gone over to the enemy. When he asks: "In the beaten way/of friendship what make you at Elsinore?" (Act II, scene 2, 269-70), the reply he receives has nothing to do with the candid friendship that they have shared in the past. Rosencrantz temporises: "To visit you, my lord. No other occasion". Hamlet gives them every chance to be honest with him, but to no avail. In what follows Rosencrantz and Guildenstern are firmly established as the King's spies. They have, in short, become totally politicised. "Nay then, I have an eye of you." Hamlet communes with himself. (Act II, scene 2, 290) But with the arrival of the players he consents for old time's sake to resume the jocular tone of their discourse. Hamlet is by no means a political naïf himself, and knows when an open rupture will be of no service to his cause. When it is time to dispose of Rosencrantz and Guildenstern he will do so without a backward glance.

Young Fortinbras apart (and since he is off stage until the very end of the action, he is not an active participant until then) Claudius is the one character who is consistently political in his outlook on life. Although directors commonly emphasise an overtly sexualised relationship between Claudius and Gertrude, there is actually nothing in what passes between them in the text to suggest that erotic passion is a powerful component in their relationship. Of course the short run up to marriage must have included wooing and seduction. But Claudius seems to have married purely as a means of consolidating his power. Nowhere in the text is it suggested that he and Gertrude behave in public as if they are sexually besotted with each other.

Claudius's attitude to Hamlet, too, is a purely political one. He cannot inhabit a world of moral outrage as Hamlet can, and sees him purely in terms of the threat to his throne. After the nunnery scene he rejects out of hand the version of Hamlet's madness that has been given to him with such assurance by Polonius.

> KING
> Love? His affections do not that way tend;
> Nor what he spake, though it lacked form a little,
> Was not like madness. There's something in his soul
> O'er which his melancholy sits on brood,
> And I do doubt the hatch and the disclose
> Will be some danger;
>
> (Act III, Scene 1, 163-8)

That Hamlet's principal emotion towards him might arise from the unlawful/incestuous/morally distasteful sex he is having with his mother never at any point occurs to Claudius. Even after the Play scene he continues to think of Hamlet as a purely political threat, and proceeds accordingly.

As Spencer points out in his note on Act III, scene 3, 8ff, though Rosencrantz and Guildenstern are by now thoroughly corrupt individuals, it does not invalidate their assessments on kingship, and its preservation as the vital component of state security. They believe what they are saying:

> GUILDENSTERN
>   The cess of majesty
> Dies not alone, but like a gulf doth draw
> What's near it with it; or 'tis a massy wheel,
> Fixed on the summit of the highest mount,
> To whose huge spokes ten thousand lesser things
> Are mortised and adjoined; which when it falls,
> Each small annexment, petty consequence,
> Attends the boisterous ruin. Never alone
> Did the king sigh, but with a general groan.
>
> (Act III, scene 3, 15-23)

An Elizabethan audience, conscious that England's monarch was drawing to the end of her life, without having provided an heir to the throne, in an era when the threat from Spain was ever present, would have been in instinctive and profound agreement with Guildenstern's assessment. The king is the vital building block of the state and its security. All other things are subordinate to his preservation.

Indeed it is a measure of the state of peril that Hamlet has manoeuvred himself into here that an audience would be silently nodding at this. The obtaining of proof to satisfy his own mind has been achieved at a great political cost. Within the play, the audience for Hamlet's theatricals is not aware of the fact that Claudius has been presented with the image of his own evil deeds, only that the King has been unwarrantedly insulted and upset. The court is (metaphorically of course) up in arms, and Hamlet has put himself in the wrong.

In that context it becomes not a failure but, I would suggest, a *necessity* that Hamlet shall fail to kill Claudius when he encounters him alone and praying. What would have been the result had he done so? Undoubtedly his arrest and confinement, perhaps immediate execution. He is a man at that point totally without a power base. Killing Claudius would simply be seen as yet another mad act from a palpably mad prince.

That does not mean that we are not thoroughly to identify with Hamlet's argument, as he stands over his uncle with drawn sword. We are to believe him, as a man inescapably of his religious milieu, when he reflects that to strike now would merely send the King to heaven, an opportunity Claudius denied to Hamlet's father. We are also meant to savour the fact that in this instance, Hamlet is led into one of his rare intellectual failures. "My words fly up, my thoughts remain below./Words without thoughts never to heaven go." (Act III, scene 3, 97-8) is Claudius's own assessment of his praying effort – i.e. God is not listening. Hamlet might have struck after all and dispatched his man to Hell.

But are we left with the gut feeling that here is an opportunity lost – something that (against all reason) we would like to see reversed? – as we undoubtedly are, however many times we may see and read *Romeo and Juliet*, in the case of the miscarried message that dooms the two lovers? I think not. It would be as if Lear, at some point before catastrophe strikes him and ultimately leads him to self-knowledge, suddenly decided to seek out Cordelia and make peace and a life with her beyond the seas. As we said earlier, the issues at stake in the play have by this point gone beyond mere revenge. Claudius must be allowed to carry on living, to carry on corrupting and doing evil if the magnitude of his eventual destruction – and of everything he stands for – is to be fully comprehended as the real meaning of *Hamlet*. And that is what he does. Hamlet is to be dispatched to England and a death by treachery. And when he outwits Claudius and returns to Denmark unscathed, Claudius has his 'Plan B' ready to hand. Laertes, himself returning to Denmark in an unthinking, vengeful mood after his father's death, is no match for Claudius's powers of suggestion. We have to admire his cunning.

> KING
>   Laertes, was your father dear to you?
>   Or are you like the painting of a sorrow,
>   A face without a heart?
> LAERTES
>   Why ask you this?
> KING
>   Not that I think you did not love your father,
>   But that I know love is begun by time,
>   And that I see, in passages of proof,
>   Time qualifies the spark and fire of it.
>   (Act IV, scene 7, 106-12)

Claudius knows his man, and his transparent impetuousness. By the time this carefully calculated speech reaches its climax

> KING
>   What would you undertake
>   To show yourself in deed your father's son
>   More than in words?

he knows exactly the kind of answer he will receive. And Laertes obliges:

> LAERTES
>   To cut his throat i'th'church!

Thus is a second plot against Hamlet hatched. And for a second time, as we shall see, it fails. Not because of any failure of political acumen in Claudius, but simply because, by this time in the play, politics –

in the shape of men who think merely politically – will not prove to be enough to resolve the great issues that the play has raised. While Shakespeare acknowledges certain political necessities – the political stability of the state being chief among them – he does not consent to a morally neutral universe.

When Hamlet found that he had killed Polonius his only regret was that he had not killed his "better", i.e. Claudius. What he had actually done was to strike the first blow in the battle to return Elsinore to decency. As so often in Shakespeare, such a moment may be cloaked in the appearance of a defeat. The fatal wounding of Cornwall in *King Lear* results, on a superficial level, merely in the death of the Duke and its perpetrator, whose body is unceremoniously thrown "upon the dunghill". It is only later seen as the first stage on the path to redemption. For Gertrude, the killing of Polonius is "a rash and bloody deed" (Act III, scene 4, 28) – as from any point of view of political commonsense it is. But Hamlet is above politics here.

> For this same lord,
> I do repent. But heaven hath pleased it so,
> To punish me with this, and this with me,
> That I must be their scourge and minister.
> (Act III, scene 4, 173-6)

This is not just conceit from Hamlet (as some of his characterisations of himself in the soliloquies manifestly are – e.g. no one really takes him at his estimation of himself as a "rogue and peasant slave"). It is far too carelessly thrown away for that. We do not have to think of Hamlet as a highly religious man (though as we have seen his thoughts operate against the backdrop of the contemporary religious ethos), but nevertheless Shakespeare makes it clear, as Kitto puts it, that "Justice is operating here". And it operates again no less surely in Hamlet's encompassing the deaths of Rosencrantz and Guildenstern, who were meant, effectively, to be his executioners. For a second time Hamlet's acumen thwarts the plot against him. It is characteristic of him that, though by and large a wholly apolitical animal, when he bestirs himself to action he is a match for any of his opponents.

Finally, right at the end of the play (one might almost say after the end of the play, since its purpose has by that time been completely worked out) the geopolitical imperatives of which we were aware at the outset of the play now reassert themselves. Fortinbras, whom we last saw going to fight a war "against some part of Poland" for "a little patch of ground/ That hath in it no profit but the name." (Act IV, scene 4, 18-19) is back. The King is dead, Hamlet is dead, Fortinbras is the man of the hour. The ship of state must be steadied and he is the man to do it. "I embrace my fortune./I have some rights of memory in this kingdom,/Which now to claim my vantage doth invite me." (Act V, scene 2, 382-4.) And he assumes the reins of government without further ado.

On the purely political level there is no better summary of this moment that that of the Polish critic Jan Kott, who wrote in the 1960s under the oppressive sway of Soviet-sponsored communism in his country, and knew all about the exercise of political power based on *la raison du plus fort*:

> Fortinbras is a young, strong and cheerful fellow. On his arrival he delivers a speech to this effect: "Take away these corpses. Hamlet was a good boy, but he is dead. Now I shall be your king I have just remembered that I happen to have certain rights to this crown." Then he smiles and is very pleased with himself.
>
> (Jan Kott, *Shakespeare Our Contemporary*,
> tr. Boleslaw Taborski, 1965)

For Fortinbras this is justifiably perceived as the truth of what has transpired. And, entering at the opportune moment with his small party of soldiers, he achieves even more than he had been agitating for at the outset of the play. The deeper truth of what has happened at Elsinore is simply not his concern.

6

Hamlet as Nemesis

Hamlet left Denmark in Act IV, sent as Claudius thought, to a convenient death in England. He returns as his nemesis. In everything he does there is now a careless vigour. There is an air almost of cheek in the way he announces his arrival to Claudius in a short note which is a clear proof to the King that his attempt on his nephew's life has failed. When we first see the returned Hamlet at Ophelia's graveside he revels in a train of philosophical thought set off by the grisly appurtenances of interment in a churchyard. Any consideration of further plots against him (which, knowing Claudius as Hamlet does, he can be sure of) are completely set aside for the moment. He and Horatio might be carefree students again as they discuss the grim fact of death, first among themselves and then with the Gravedigger. And when he announces himself to the funeral party that accompanies Ophelia to her final resting place, Hamlet does so with majestic self assurance. "This is I,/Hamlet the Dane." (Act V, scene 1, 253-4.) There is only one man in Denmark who should be allowed to style himself thus – the King himself. In assuming the title Hamlet is effectively arrogating to himself the rule of Denmark.

His subsequent account to Horatio of the manner in which he outwitted Rosencrantz and Guildenstern, the luckless executants of Claudius's plot against him is, likewise, a thing of vigorous narrative interest. And when Horatio appears to demur over the impending death of their two erstwhile student comrades, Hamlet brushes him aside: "Why, man, they did make love to this employment./They are not near my conscience." (Act V, scene 2, 57-8.) Simply, they have become agents of the king. They have been complicit in evil, and we are to see their deaths, as Hamlet does, as poetic justice. As Cruttwell points out, by this stage "Hamlet is at war". Hamlet now clear-sightedly sees what the issue between him and Claudius must be. There is a sense of urgency that has been lacking up to this point in his deliberations.

> And with such cozenage – is't not perfect conscience
> To quit him with this arm? And is't not to be damned
> To let this canker of our nature come
> In further evil?
>
> (Act V, scene 2, 67-70)

As it happens, it will be at Claudius's and not Hamlet's initiative that this end will be encompassed. A plot to kill him has already been discussed by the King and Laertes (Act IV, scene 7, 133ff). And surely, if there were still any residue of sympathy for Laertes in us, on the score of his grief for his father's and sister's deaths, it must be dispelled by the alacrity with which he not only falls in with Claudius's design for a rigged fencing match, but improves on it. Claudius counts on Hamlet's being, as he only too well knows: "Most generous, and free from all contriving". In this atmosphere of trust Laertes may "with a little shuffling ... choose/A sword unbated, and, in a pass of practice,/Requite him for your father." In other words, Claudius can arrange that one of the rapiers among those from which each combatant will choose his weapon has no button on its end, but is a sharp, potentially lethal, point. Laertes will choose this one. And he will go one better: "I will do't,/And for that purpose I'll anoint my sword./I bought an unction of a mountebank/So mortal ..." Shakespeare's viewpoint is crystal clear here. There will be something "shuffling" about the business. Laertes has bought his poison "of a mountebank". What "noble youth" as Hamlet generously assesses Laertes to be, buys poisons from a quack doctor to use in case his much vaunted swordplay fails him?

It is perhaps worth stepping aside for a moment to examine the terms of the impending fencing match, since they have caused such confusion. Shakespeare has the foppish courtier Osrick explain them to Hamlet, but they are not the less interesting for that. They would, of course, have been of intense interest to a knowledgeable Elizabethan audience, and there is no reason not to try to understand them ourselves – especially as they bear importantly on the course of the match as far as it is permitted to go, *as* a match, before the rules are dispensed with and it becomes a scuffle to the death. Osrick's explanation

> The King, sir, hath laid, sir, that in a dozen passes between yourself and him he shall not exceed you three hits. He hath laid on twelve for nine;
>
> (Act V, Scene 2, 162-5)

has puzzled many commentators. Even the normally sagacious Dr Johnson confessed himself unable to understand how in a contest of a dozen passes, one participant could win 12-9, as is apparently suggested here. But the passage can *only* make sense if the three references to "him", "he" and "He" are all understood as applying to Laertes. "Twelve for nine", then, has nothing to do with a possible scoreline. Simply, "He" (Laertes, not the king) has stipulated that the contest shall consist of twelve passes, not (the presumably normal?) nine. This may be because Laertes fancies that the unfit scholar Hamlet will tire over the duration of a longer bout, even if he gets ahead at the beginning. The king, meanwhile, has wagered that at the end of these twelve passes Laertes will not have managed to get three ahead. In other words, if Hamlet scores five hits he wins the match, since even if he won all the rest Laertes could only possibly be two up at 7-5. And, in the event, with Hamlet winning the first two and drawing the third, the contest – and with it his and Claudius's plot – is entering a crisis period for Laertes. There are nine more passes left. Hamlet has only to win another two and draw one more, and the match will be over, without Laertes' having a chance to lay a touch on Hamlet with his unbated, poisoned point.

Interestingly, Shakespeare makes it clear that in fencing, as in much else in life, Hamlet will exercise an effortless superiority. When the match is mooted I think we feel, as an anxious Horatio does: "You will lose this wager my lord." (Act V, sscene 2, 202) Hamlet reassures him to the contrary. But his assurance of his superiority to Laertes in fencing is of merely secondary importance to him here. Does he suspect that the match is cover for another plot against his life? Possibly. But he is, in any event, already gazing into an outcome beyond that. While Horatio continues to fuss affectionately around him, begging for his consent to ask to have the match called off or postponed, Hamlet shrugs off the suggestion in terms which appear to regard his fate as being not important in itself, but as being merely part of a general destiny.

> The readiness is all. Since no man knows
> of aught he leaves, what is't to leave betimes?
> Let be.

(Act V, scene 2, 216-18)

We are reminded irresistibly of similar lines from Act V, scene 2 of another play still several years in the future at the time Shakespeare was finishing writing *Hamlet*. "The readiness is all" is inescapably echoed in *King Lear* by Edgar's admonition "Ripeness is all" to his blinded father, Gloucester, as events move towards their end in that play too. In both cases catastrophe is impending, and the good will perish along with the wicked. But Man, the philosopher, will have studied how to die.

In the final whirlwind of the denouement, it is suddenly as if all the power of Hamlet's mind is concentrated into a scene of the most violent action. With all the principal players of the drama – Hamlet, his mother, the King, Laertes – now assembled it seems fitting that the punishment of Claudius can at last take place. At any time prior to this moment it would have seemed merely an act of revenge. Now, as the instrument which finally ends the reign of wickedness, Hamlet seems to be a part of that destiny which, as he earlier recognised, "shapes our ends".

In this context Claudius's death at Hamlet's hands is seen not merely as discharging the Ghost's injunction, but is visible to all as symbolic of the final defeat of the evil that has beset Elsinore, spreading throughout every fibre of the Danish state and dragging down the innocent, and the merely supine, along with the bad. Men at last know themselves.

At the end there can be forgiveness for Laertes, and it is freely given by Hamlet. There can even be pity for Gertrude whose defective perception has made her, in the ultimate analysis, not so much the king's lover and wife, as one of his victims. Indeed, one of Claudius's most startling crimes against decency has been to destroy Hamlet's love for his own mother. At the end, as she dies in the agonies of poison, Hamlet can muster for her only the barely sympathetic "Wretched Queen, adieu!"

For Claudius, as the embodiment of these evils, there cannot, realistically, be such a thing as forgiveness. In the last moments of his life Laertes, who has been gulled, like so many in the play, into becoming one of Claudius's creatures, recognises this truth, in his verdict on the king's death: "He is justly served." (Act V, scene 2, 321.) And the nature of Claudius's death, killed not by a sword thrust, as might befit the denouement of a tragedy, but by having his mouth prised open and poison forced down his throat by the nephew whose death he has long sought, seems only to underline this. His dying in this manner, rather like a farm animal having a drench (lethal, in this case) administered to it, makes for a compellingly grisly scene. He will be neither missed nor long remembered. The contrast with the death of Hamlet could not be more pointed.

HORATIO
Now cracks a noble heart. Good night, sweet Prince,
And flights of angels sing thee to thy rest!
(Act V, scene 2, 353-4)

It is one of the most memorable leave-takings in literature.

As happens so often in Shakespeare, lesser men will inherit the earth. There is a decent, if somewhat uninvolved, nod in the direction of Hamlet's qualities from Fortinbras.

For he was likely, had he been put on,
To have proved most royal.
(Act V, scene 2, 391-2)

And it is on with the business. The 'new' Denmark will be run by the pragmatist. It will have no ghosts. It will have no antic dispositions. It will be no place for the soaring imagination of a Hamlet.

Further Reading

Critical and biographical studies

A.C. Bradley: *Shakespearean Tragedy* (Macmillan, 1904). Influential in his day for the moral seriousness of his criticism, Bradley fell out of fashion from the mid-20th century onwards. But his qualities of earnestness and decency are being recognised anew. His unshakeable view of an essentially 'morbid' Hamlet perhaps makes his interpretation of this play less successful than that of the other tragedies. But he is always worth reading.

Samuel Taylor Coleridge: *Lectures 1818*, collected in *Samuel Taylor Coleridge: Shakespearean Criticism*, ed. Thomas Middleton Raysor (Everyman's Library, 1974); also in *The Romantics on Shakespeare*, ed. Jonathan Bate (Penguin, 1992), which also contains essays by Schlegel, Hazlitt, Lamb and Keats. The chief of the English Romantic interpreters of Hamlet's character, Coleridge is far too intelligent for even his wilder assertions to be dismissed out of hand, and his opinions have remained influential on both critical estimation and stage performance of *Hamlet*.

Edited by Martin Coyle: *Hamlet* (Palgrave, 1992). A selection of contemporary critical essays in the paperback series New Casebooks. These survey recent and current developments in analysis of the play, with amusing and forceful comments on the shortcomings of Gertrude and Ophelia as perceived by such feminists as Marilyn French and Elaine Showalter.

Patrick Cruttwell: *The Morality of Hamlet – 'Sweet Prince' or 'Arrant Knave'?* (first published in *Stratford-upon Avon Studies 5*, 1963, but readily accessible in the paperback Casebook Series volume

Shakespeare: Hamlet, 1968 – see below). Cruttwell's account of the play gets to the heart of its problems in a way many longer studies fail to do.

Andrew Dickson: *The Rough Guide to Shakespeare* (2005). An intelligently compiled reference work that provides interesting insights into each of the plays, from the standpoint of reader, playgoer and film buff.

Philip Edwards: *Tragic Balance in Hamlet* (*Shakespeare Survey, 36*, 1983). A useful discussion of the issues that have dominated criticism of the play and its protagonist.

Harley Granville-Barker: *Prefaces to Shakespeare: Third Series* (Sidgwick & Jackson, 1937). The consummate man of the theatre, Granville-Barker has the playwright's and director's understanding of the play's technical difficulties, and his astute eye for detail of stage business and for characterisation, once thought old-fashioned, can be savoured these days with fresh pleasure and profit.

Samuel Johnson: *Mr Johnson's Preface to his Edition of Shakespeare's Plays* (1765). This is the first sustained critical analysis of Shakespeare's plays, achieving a status that has endured, long after the edition it accompanied was superseded. It is full of wise insights. Even when we do not agree with Johnson's conclusions, they can never be dismissed. Available in modern editions.

Edited by John Jump: *Shakespeare: Hamlet* (Macmillan, 1968, 1990) A good selection of essays on *Hamlet*, ranging from the 18th to the mid-20th century in the extremely useful paperback Casebook Series.

William Kerrigan: *Hamlet's Perfection* (Johns Hopkins University Press, 1994). A *cri de coeur*, calling for a return from the aridity afflicting so much of the post-modern commentary on *Hamlet* to the humane standards which its author sees as particularly residing in the critics of the Bradley era.

H.D.F. Kitto: *Form and Meaning in Drama* (Methuen, 1956). This is a study of six dramas by Aeschylus and Sophocles, from which standpoint Kitto makes comparisons between the 5th-century Attic stage and Elizabethan theatre. It has a long final chapter on *Hamlet,* seen in the light of Shakespeare's great precursors. Kitto's thorough understanding of what tragedy is brings unrivalled insights to his commentary on the play.

G. Wilson Knight: *The Wheel of Fire* (OUP, 1930). As in his essay on *King Lear* (from a speech of whose protagonist this celebrated study takes its title), the stalwart Christian Wilson Knight sometimes gives the impression of not really having a strong enough stomach for Shakespeare. In a chapter 'Hamlet Reconsidered' (1947) added to later editions of the book, he attempted to revise his 1930 verdict ("Hamlet is an element of evil in the state of Denmark"), but still could not find the play's protagonist a sympathetic figure.

L.C. Knights: *An Approach to Hamlet* (Chatto and Windus, 1960, reprinted in harness with *Some Shakespearean Themes*, Peregrine Books, 1966). Knights does not really approve of Hamlet, but his analysis of the protagonist's revulsion for his mother's sins offers interesting insights.

Jan Kott: *Shakespeare Our Contemporary* (Methuen, 1965). Kott wrote, and directed drama, in his native Poland in an era when it was a police state dominated by its Russian neighbour. He brings an understanding of the naked brutalities of power politics to everything he writes.

August Wilhelm Schlegel: *Lectures on Dramatic Art and Literature* (given in Vienna, 1808, published, 1809–11). Part of a wide-ranging study of the dramatic literature of Europe from classical Greek tragedy to Schlegel's contemporaries. An early exemplar of the 'Romantic' view of Hamlet's character, though none the worse for that, Schlegel is particularly good on Shakespeare, whom he greatly admired. He produced some remarkable translations, which gave the dramatist an enduring popularity in Germany. Available in modern critical anthologies.

John Dover Wilson: *What Happens in Hamlet* (CUP, 1935). As its title boldly asserts, this is a thorough study of the play which leaves few stones unturned. Although one does not have to agree with all its conclusions it is a must for any student of the play.

GREENWICH EXCHANGE BOOKS

STUDENT GUIDE LITERARY SERIES

The Greenwich Exchange Student Guide Literary Series is a collection of essays on major or contemporary serious writers in English and selected European languages. The series is for the student, the teacher and 'common readers' and is an ideal resource for libraries. The *Times Educational Supplement* praised these books, saying, "The style of [this series] has a pressure of meaning behind it. Readers should learn from that ... If art is about selection, perception and taste, then this is it."

(ISBN prefix 978-1-871551 applies unless marked*, when the prefix 978-1-906075 applies.)

The series includes:
Antonin Artaud by Lee Jamieson (98-3)
W.H. Auden by Stephen Wade (36-5)
Jane Austen by Pat Levy (89-1)
Honoré de Balzac by Wendy Mercer (48-8)
William Blake by Peter Davies (27-3)
The Brontës by Peter Davies (24-2)
Robert Browning by John Lucas (59-4)
Lord Byron by Andrew Keanie (83-9)
Samuel Taylor Coleridge by Andrew Keanie (64-8)
Joseph Conrad by Martin Seymour-Smith (18-1)
William Cowper by Michael Thorn (25-9)
Charles Dickens by Robert Giddings (26-9)
Emily Dickinson by Marnie Pomeroy (68-6)
John Donne by Sean Haldane (23-5)
Ford Madox Ford by Anthony Fowles (63-1)
The Stagecraft of Brian Friel by David Grant (74-7)
Robert Frost by Warren Hope (70-9)
Patrick Hamilton by John Harding (99-0)
Thomas Hardy by Sean Haldane (33-4)
Seamus Heaney by Warren Hope (37-2)
Joseph Heller by Anthony Fowles (84-6)
Gerard Manley Hopkins by Sean Sheehan (77-3)
James Joyce by Michael Murphy (73-0)
Philip Larkin by Warren Hope (35-8)
Laughter in the Dark – The Plays of Joe Orton by Arthur Burke (56-3)
George Orwell by Warren Hope (42-6)

Sylvia Plath by Marnie Pomeroy (88-4)
Poets of the First World War by John Greening (79-2)
Philip Roth by Paul McDonald (72-3)
Shakespeare's *A Midsummer Night's Dream* by Matt Simpson (90-7)
Shakespeare's *Hamlet* by Peter Davies (12-5)*
Shakespeare's *King Lear* by Peter Davies (95-2)
Shakespeare's *Macbeth* by Matt Simpson (69-3)
Shakespeare's *The Merchant of Venice* by Alan Ablewhite (96-9)
Shakespeare's *Much Ado About Nothing* by Matt Simpson (01-9)*
Shakespeare's Non-Dramatic Poetry by Martin Seymour-Smith (22-6)
Shakespeare's *Othello* by Matt Simpson (71-6)
Shakespeare's Second Tetralogy: *Richard II – Henry V* by John Lucas (97-6)
Shakespeare's Sonnets by Martin Seymour-Smith (38-9)
Shakespeare's *The Tempest* by Matt Simpson (75-4)
Shakespeare's *Twelfth Night* by Matt Simpson (86-0)
Shakespeare's *The Winter's Tale* by John Lucas (80-3)
Tobias Smollett by Robert Giddings (21-1)
Alfred, Lord Tennyson by Michael Thorn (20-4)
Dylan Thomas by Peter Davies (78-5)
William Wordsworth by Andrew Keanie (57-0)
W.B. Yeats by John Greening (34-1)

FOCUS Series
Emily Brontë's *Wuthering Heights* by Matt Simpson (10-1)*
George Eliot's *Middlemarch* by John Axon (06-4)*
T.S. Eliot's *The Waste Land* by Matt Simpson (09-5)*
Michael Frayn's *Spies* by Angela Topping (08-8)*
Thomas Hardy: *Poems of 1912–13* by John Greening (04-0)*
The Poetry of Ted Hughes by John Greening (05-7)*
The Poetry of Tony Harrison by Sean Sheehan (15-6)*
James Joyce's *A Portrait of the Artist as a Young Man* by
    Matt Simpson (07-1)*

LITERATURE & BIOGRAPHY

Matthew Arnold and 'Thyrsis' *by Patrick Carill Connolly*
Matthew Arnold (1822-1888) was a leading poet, intellect and aesthete of
the Victorian epoch. He is now best known for his strictures as a literary
and cultural critic, and educationist. After a long period of neglect, his
views have come in for a revaluation. Arnold's poetry remains less well

known, yet his poems and his understanding of poetry, which defied the conventions of his time, were central to his achievement. The author traces Arnold's intellectual and poetic development, showing how his poetry gathers its meanings from a lifetime's study of European literature and philosophy. Connolly's unique exegesis of 'Thyrsis' draws upon a wide-ranging analysis of the pastoral and its associated myths in both classical and native cultures. This study shows lucidly and in detail how Arnold encouraged the intense reflection of the mind on the subject placed before it, believing in " ... the all importance of the choice of the subject, the necessity of accurate observation; and subordinate character of expression."

Patrick Carill Connolly gained his English degree at Reading University and taught English literature abroad for a number of years before returning to Britain. He is now a civil servant living in London.

2004 • 180 pages • ISBN 978-1-871551-61-7

The Author, the Book and the Reader *by Robert Giddings*
This collection of essays analyses the effects of changing technology and the attendant commercial pressures on literary styles and subject matter. Authors covered include Charles Dickens, Tobias Smollett, Mark Twain, Dr Johnson and John le Carré.

1991 • 220 pages • illustrated • ISBN 978-1-871551-01-3

Norman Cameron *by Warren Hope*
Cameron's poetry was admired by Auden; celebrated by Dylan Thomas; valued by Robert Graves. He was described by Martin Seymour-Smith as "one of ... the most rewarding and pure poets of his generation ..." and is at last given a full-length biography. This eminently sociable man, who had periods of darkness and despair, wrote little poetry by comparison with others of his time, but always of a consistently high quality – imaginative and profound.

Warren Hope is a poet, a critic and university lecturer. He lives and works in Philadelphia, where he raised his family.

2000 • 226 pages • ISBN 978-1-871551-05-1

Aleister Crowley and the Cult of Pan *by Paul Newman*
Few more nightmarish figures stalk English literature than Aleister Crowley (1875-1947), poet, magician, mountaineer and agent provocateur. In this groundbreaking study, Paul Newman dives into the occult mire of Crowley's works and fishes out gems and grotesqueries that are by turns ethereal, sublime, pornographic and horrifying. Like Oscar Wilde before him, Crowley stood in "symbolic relationship to his age" and to contemporaries like Rupert Brooke, G.K. Chesterton and the Portuguese modernist,

Fernando Pessoa. An influential exponent of the cult of the Great God Pan, his essentially 'pagan' outlook was shared by major European writers as well as English novelists like E.M. Forster, D.H. Lawrence and Arthur Machen.

Paul Newman lives in Cornwall. Editor of the literary magazine *Abraxas*, he has written over ten books.

2004 • 222 pages • ISBN 978-1-871551-66-2

John Dryden *by Anthony Fowles*
Of all the poets of the Augustan age, John Dryden was the most worldly. Anthony Fowles traces Dryden's evolution from 'wordsmith' to major poet. This critical study shows a poet of vigour and technical panache whose art was forged in the heat and battle of a turbulent polemical and pamphleteering age. Although Dryden's status as a literary critic has long been established, Fowles draws attention to his neglected achievements as a translator of poetry. He deals also with the less well-known aspects of Dryden's work – his plays and occasional pieces.

Born in London and educated at the Universities of Oxford and Southern California, Anthony Fowles began his career in film-making before becoming an author of film and television scripts and more than twenty books. Readers will welcome the many contemporary references to novels and film with which Fowles illuminates the life and work of this decisively influential English poetic voice.

2003 • 292 pages • ISBN 978-1-871551-58-7

The Good That We Do *by John Lucas*
John Lucas' book blends fiction, biography and social history in order to tell the story of his grandfather, Horace Kelly. Headteacher of a succession of elementary schools in impoverished areas of London, 'Hod' Kelly was also a keen cricketer, a devotee of the music hall, and included among his friends the great trade union leader Ernest Bevin. In telling the story of his life, Lucas has provided a fascinating range of insights into the lives of ordinary Londoners from the First World War until the outbreak of the Second World War. Threaded throughout is an account of such people's hunger for education, and of the different ways government, church and educational officialdom ministered to that hunger. *The Good That We Do* is both a study of one man and of a period when England changed, drastically and forever.

John Lucas is Professor Emeritus of the Universities of Loughborough and Nottingham Trent. He is the author of numerous works of a critical and scholarly nature and has published eight collections of poetry.

2001 • 214 pages • ISBN 978-1-871551-54-9

D.H. Lawrence: The Nomadic Years, 1919-1930 *by Philip Callow*
This book provides a fresh insight into Lawrence's art as well as his life. Candid about the relationship between Lawrence and his wife, it shows nevertheless the strength of the bond between them. If no other book persuaded the reader of Lawrence's greatness, this does.
Philip Callow was born in Birmingham and studied engineering and teaching before he turned to writing. He has published 14 novels, several collections of short stories and poems, a volume of autobiography, and biographies on the lives of Chekhov, Cezanne, Robert Louis Stevenson, Walt Whitman and Van Gogh all of which have received critical acclaim. His biography of D.H. Lawrence's early years, *Son and Lover*, was widely praised.
2006 • 226 pages • ISBN 978-1-871551-82-2

Liar! Liar!: Jack Kerouac – Novelist *by R.J. Ellis*
The fullest study of Jack Kerouac's fiction to date. It is the first book to devote an individual chapter to every one of his novels. *On the Road*, *Visions of Cody* and *The Subterraneans* are reread in-depth, in a new and exciting way. *Visions of Gerard* and *Doctor Sax* are also strikingly reinterpreted, as are other daringly innovative writings, like 'The Railroad Earth' and his "try at a spontaneous *Finnegans Wake*" – *Old Angel Midnight*. Neglected writings, such as *Tristessa* and *Big Sur*, are also analysed, alongside better-known novels such as *Dharma Bums* and *Desolation Angels*.
R.J. Ellis is Senior Lecturer in English at Nottingham Trent University.
1999 • 294 pages • ISBN 978-1-871551-53-2

Musical Offering *by Yolanthe Leigh*
In a series of vivid sketches, anecdotes and reflections, Yolanthe Leigh tells the story of her growing up in the Poland of the 1930s and the Second World War. These are poignant episodes of a child's first encounters with both the enchantments and the cruelties of the world; and from a later time, stark memories of the brutality of the Nazi invasion, and the hardships of student life in Warsaw under the Occupation. But most of all this is a record of inward development; passages of remarkable intensity and simplicity describe the girl's response to religion, to music, and to her discovery of philosophy.
Yolanthe Leigh was formerly a Lecturer in Philosophy at Reading University.
2000 • 56 pages • ISBN: 978-1-871551-46-4

In Pursuit of Lewis Carroll *by Raphael Shaberman*
Sherlock Holmes and the author uncover new evidence in their investigations into the mysterious life and writing of Lewis Carroll. They examine

published works by Carroll that have been overlooked by previous commentators. A newly-discovered poem, almost certainly by Carroll, is published here.

Amongst many aspects of Carroll's highly complex personality, this book explores his relationship with his parents, numerous child friends, and the formidable Mrs Liddell, mother of the immortal Alice. Raphael Shaberman was a founder member of the Lewis Carroll Society and a teacher of autistic children.

1994 • 118 pages • illustrated • ISBN 978-1-871551-13-6

Poetry in Exile: A study of the poetry of W.H. Auden, Joseph Brodsky & George Szirtes *by Michael Murphy*

"Michael Murphy discriminates the forms of exile and expatriation with the shrewdness of the cultural historian, the acuity of the literary critic, and the subtlety of a poet alert to the ways language and poetic form embody the precise contours of experience. His accounts of Auden, Brodsky and Szirtes not only cast much new light on the work of these complex and rewarding poets, but are themselves a pleasure to read." *Stan Smith, Research Professor in Literary Studies, Nottingham Trent University.*

Michael Murphy is a poet and critic. He teaches English literature at Liverpool Hope University College.

2004 • 266 pages • ISBN 978-1-871551-76-1

Wordsworth and Coleridge: Views from the Meticulous to the Sublime *by Andrew Keanie*

For a long time the received view of the collaborative relationship between Wordsworth and Coleridge has been that Wordsworth was the efficient producer of more finished poetic statements (most notably his long, autobiographical poem *The Prelude*) and Coleridge, however extraordinary he was as a thinker and a talker, left behind more intolerably diffuse and fragmented works. *Wordsworth and Coleridge: Views from the Meticulous to the Sublime* examines the issue from a number of different critical vantage points, reassessing the poets' inextricable achievements, and rediscovering their legacy.

Andrew Keanie is a lecturer at the University of Ulster. He is the author of articles on William Wordsworth, Samuel Taylor Coleridge and Hartley Coleridge. He has written three books for the Greenwich Exchange *Student Guide Literary Series* on Wordsworth, Coleridge and Byron.

2007 • 206 pages • ISBN 978-1-871551-87-7 (Hardback)

POETRY

Adam's Thoughts in Winter *by Warren Hope*
Warren Hope's poems have appeared from time to time in a number of
literary periodicals, pamphlets and anthologies on both sides of the Atlantic.
They appeal to lovers of poetry everywhere. His poems are brief, clear,
frequently lyrical, characterised by wit, but often distinguished by
tenderness. The poems gathered in this first book-length collection counter
the brutalising ethos of contemporary life, speaking of, and for, the virtues
of modesty, honesty and gentleness in an individual, memorable way.
2000 • 46 pages • ISBN 978-1-871551-40-2

Baudelaire: Les Fleurs du Mal *Translated by F.W. Leakey*
Selected poems from *Les Fleurs du Mal* are translated with parallel French
texts and are designed to be read with pleasure by readers who have no
French as well as those who are practised in the French language.
F.W. Leakey was Professor of French in the University of London. As a
scholar, critic and teacher he specialised in the work of Baudelaire for 50
years and published a number of books on the poet.
2001 • 152 pages • ISBN 978-1-871551-10-5

'The Last Blackbird' and other poems by Ralph Hodgson *edited and
introduced by John Harding*
Ralph Hodgson (1871-1962) was a poet and illustrator whose most
influential and enduring work appeared to great acclaim just prior to, and
during, the First World War. His work is imbued with a spiritual passion for
the beauty of creation and the mystery of existence. This new selection
brings together, for the first time in 40 years, some of the most beautiful
and powerful 'hymns to life' in the English language.
John Harding lives in London. He is a freelance writer and teacher and is
Ralph Hodgson's biographer.
2004 • 70 pages • ISBN 978-871551-81-5

Lines from the Stone Age *by Sean Haldane*
Reviewing Sean Haldane's 1992 volume *Desire in Belfast*, Robert Nye wrote
in *The Times* that "Haldane can be sure of his place among the English
poets." This place is not yet a conspicuous one, mainly because his early
volumes appeared in Canada, and because he has earned his living by other
means than literature. Despite this, his poems have always had their circle
of readers. The 60 previously unpublished poems of *Lines from the Stone
Age* – "lines of longing, terror, pride, lust and pain" – may widen this circle.
2000 • 52 pages • ISBN 978-1-871551-39-6

Lipstick *by Maggie Butt*

Lipstick is Maggie Butt's debut collection of poems and marks the entrance of a voice at once questioning and self-assured. She believes that poetry should be the tip of the stiletto which slips between the ribs directly into the heart. The poems of *Lipstick* are often deceptively simple, unafraid of focusing on such traditional themes as time, loss and love through a range of lenses and personae. Maggie Butt is capable of speaking in the voice of an 11th-century stonemason, a Himalayan villager, a 13-year-old anorexic. When writing of such everyday things as nylon sheets, jumble sales, X-rays or ginger beer, she brings to her subjects a dry humour and an acute insight. But beyond the intimate and domestic, her poems cover the world, from Mexico to Russia; they deal with war, with the resilience of women, and, most of all, with love.

Maggie Butt is head of Media and Communication at Middlesex University, London, where she has taught Creative Writing since 1990.

2007 • 72 pages • ISBN 978-1-871551-94-5

Martin Seymour-Smith – Collected Poems *edited by Peter Davies*

To the general public Martin Seymour-Smith (1928-1998) is known as a distinguished literary biographer, notably of Robert Graves, Rudyard Kipling and Thomas Hardy. To such figures as John Dover Wilson, William Empson, Stephen Spender and Anthony Burgess, he was regarded as one of the most independently-minded scholars of his generation, through his pioneering critical edition of Shakespeare's *Sonnets*, and his magisterial *Guide to Modern World Literature*.

To his fellow poets, Graves, James Reeves, C.H. Sisson and Robert Nye – he was first and foremost a poet. As this collection demonstrates, at the centre of the poems is a passionate engagement with Man, his sexuality and his personal relationships.

2006 • 182 pages • ISBN 978-1-871551-47-1

Shakespeare's Sonnets *by Martin Seymour-Smith*

Martin Seymour-Smith's outstanding achievement lies in the field of literary biography and criticism. In 1963 he produced his comprehensive edition, in the old spelling, of *Shakespeare's Sonnets* (here revised and corrected by himself and Peter Davies in 1998). With its landmark introduction and its brilliant critical commentary on each sonnet, it was praised by William Empson and John Dover Wilson. Stephen Spender said of him "I greatly admire Martin Seymour-Smith for the independence of his views and the great interest of his mind"; and both Robert Graves and Anthony Burgess described him as the leading critic of his time. His exegesis of the *Sonnets* remains unsurpassed.

2001 • 194 pages • ISBN 978-1-871551-38-9

The Rain and the Glass *by Robert Nye*
When Robert Nye's first poems were published, G.S. Fraser declared in the *Times Literary Supplement*: "Here is a proper poet, though it is hard to see how the larger literary public (greedy for flattery of their own concerns) could be brought to recognize that. But other proper poets – how many of them are left? – will recognize one of themselves." Since then Nye has become known to a large public for his novels, especially *Falstaff* (1976), winner of the Hawthornden Prize and The Guardian Fiction Prize, and *The Late Mr Shakespeare* (1998). But his true vocation has always been poetry, and it is as a poet that he is best known to his fellow poets. This book contains all the poems Nye has written since his *Collected Poems* of 1995, together with his own selection from that volume. An introduction, telling the story of his poetic beginnings, affirms Nye's unfashionable belief in inspiration, as well as defining that quality of unforced truth which distinguishes the best of his work: "I have spent my life trying to write poems, but the poems gathered here came mostly when I was not."
2005 • 132 pages • ISBN 978-1-871551-41-9

Wilderness *by Martin Seymour-Smith*
This is Martin Seymour-Smith's first publication of his poetry for more than twenty years. This collection of 36 poems is a fearless account of an inner life of love, frustration, guilt, laughter and the celebration of others. He is best known to the general public as the author of the controversial and bestselling *Hardy* (1994).
1994 • 52 pages • ISBN 978-1-871551-08-2

EDUCATION

Making School Work *by Andy Buck*
Full of practical examples, this book sets out a range of strategies for successful school leadership. It provides examples of tried and tested ideas to use when tackling some of the key challenges facing every school leader: This book aims to offer readers a range of practical approaches to both policy and leadership style, based around a series of case studies and school-based policies. Each chapter examines a key challenge facing school leaders and provides practical ideas and strategies that have been shown to work in schools.
A geography teacher since 1987, Andy Bucks' experience has included working as a head of department, head of year, deputy head and two headships, all in London schools.
2007 • 142 pages • ISBN 978-1-871551-52-5

Story: The Heart of the Matter *ed. Dr Maggie Butt*
What can't we get enough of? Food? Sex? Alcohol? Stories? We devour
hundreds of stories every day in television news, magazines, novels, movies,
jokes, plays, newspapers, and we never get tired of them. Stories always
leave us hungry for more. In this book, 15 established writers explore their
own practice and ideas about storymaking. These novelists, journalists,
poets, screenwriters, playwrights, documentary makers, oral storytellers
and stand-up comics are also leading academics in Creative Writing and
Journalism in UK universities. What do they have in common? Story.Their
examinations of storymaking shed new light on what different forms, media
and genres have in common. These writers don't tell you how to write a
play or novel or poem, but they offer personal insights which are the fruit
of years of experience. They share some of the ways to create that all-
important connection between the idea and the audience – how to make the
magic happen.
2007 • 180 pages • ISBN 978-1-871551-93-8

HISTORICAL FACTION

The Secret Life of Elizabeth I *by Paul Doherty*
A detective story with a difference – tracking down the real Elizabeth I –
capturing the atmosphere of Elizabethan and Jacobean England, with
stunning results. Paul Doherty's original research shows Elizabeth I of
England to be a strongwilled, brilliant ruler but also a woman with deep
passions and fervent attachments. The lady-in-waiting describes the
passionate relationship between Elizabeth and Robert Dudley, later Earl of
Leicester. She reveals evidence about the strange death of Dudley's wife,
the very physical relationship between Elizabeth and Dudley, and the
stunning revelation that they had a son, Arthur Dudley, seized by the Spanish
in 1587.
Paul Doherty is an internationally renowned author. He studied history at
Liverpool and Oxford Universities, gaining his doctorate at Oxford. He is
now the headmaster of a very successful London school. First in the series
published by Greenwich Exchange.
2006 • 210 pages • ISBN 978-1-871551-85-3 (Hardback)

Death of the Red King *by Paul Doherty*
Was William Rufus, the Red King, accidentally killed by one of his own
men while hunting or is there a more chilling interpretation of his death?
Doherty demonstrates that the Red King's death is highly suspect. Walter
Tirel has been cast as the villain of the piece. However, through the eyes of

Anselm the great philosopher, this faction develops a quite different version of his death.

Second in the series published by Greenwich Exchange.

2006 • 190 pages • ISBN 978-1-871551-92-1 (Hardback)

BUSINESS

English Language Skills *by Vera Hughes*

If you want to be sure, (as a student, or in your business or personal life), that your written English is correct, this book is for you. Vera Hughes' aim is to help you to remember the basic rules of spelling, grammar and punctuation. 'Noun', 'verb', 'subject', 'object' and 'adjective' are the only technical terms used. The book teaches the clear, accurate English required by the business and office world. It coaches acceptable current usage and makes the rules easier to remember.

Vera Hughes was a civil servant and is a trainer and author of training manuals.

2002 • 142 pages • ISBN 978-1-871551-60-0